LIVING GREEN
Effortlessly

• • •

Simple Choices for a Better Home

LIVING GREEN
Effortlessly

• • •

Simple Choices for a Better Home

Marla Esser Cloos

MyHome Press

Living Green Effortlessly: Simple Choices for a Better Home
MyHome Press, a Service of the National Association of Home Builders

Elizabeth M. Rich	*Director, Book Publishing*
Sherrye Landrum	*Book Editor*
anis riana | 9 green studio	*Cover Design*
pixiedesign, llc	*Composition*

Marla Esser Cloos	*Photographers*
Abby Hudson	
Tony Pratte	
Shutterstock	

King Printing Company, Inc.	*Printing*

Gerald M. Howard	*NAHB Chief Executive Officer*
Lakisha A. Woods, CAE	*Senior Vice President and Chief Marketing Officer*

Disclaimer

This publication provides accurate information on the subject matter covered. The publisher is selling it with the understanding that the publisher is not providing legal, accounting, or other professional service. If you need legal advice or other expert assistance, obtain the services of a qualified professional experienced in the subject matter involved. The NAHB has used commercially reasonable efforts to ensure that the contents of this volume are complete and appear without error; however the NAHB makes no representations or warranties regarding the accuracy and completeness of this document's contents. The NAHB specifically disclaims any implied warranties of merchantability or fitness for a particular purpose. The NAHB shall not be liable for any loss of profit or any other commercial damages, including but not limited to incidental, special, consequential or other damages. Reference herein to any specific commercial products, process, or service by trade name, trademark, manufacturer, or otherwise does not necessarily constitute or imply its endorsement, recommendation, or favored status by the NAHB. The views and opinions of the author expressed in this publication do not necessarily state or reflect those of the NAHB, and they shall not be used to advertise or endorse a product.

Printed in the United States of America

20 19 18 17   1 2 3 4 5

ISBN: 978-0-86718-752-6
eISBN: 978-0-86718-753-3

Cataloging-in-Publication Information
Library of Congress CIP information available on request.

For further information, please contact:
National Association of Home Builders
1201 15th Street, NW
Washington, DC 20005-2800
800-223-2665

Visit us online at BuilderBooks.com

Table of Contents

• • •

About the Author vii

Acknowledgments ix

Introduction 1

1. What IS an Everyday Green Home? 7

2. Your Comfort, Health, and Safety:
   Start Where You Live 21

3. Energy Efficiencies: How Can You
   Be Comfortable and Get the Most
   for Your Energy Dollars? 35

4. What Goes IN Your Home:
   What to Think About, What to
   Look For, What to Choose. 67

5. Landscaping 79

6. Maintain and Document so You
   Can Rely on Your Home 89

7. Building (or Renovating to Achieve)
   a Certified Green Home. 119

Resources. 133

About the Author

• • •

MARLA ESSER CLOOS, THE GREEN HOME COACH, is an NAHB Master Certified Green Professional, LEED AP and Missouri Women Business Enterprise. She is the founder and co-host of the Green Gab Podcast on iTunes and GreenHomeCoach.com. You can find her blogging on Green Home Coach and Proud Green Home. Her articles have appeared in *Green Home Builder, Building Women* and *The Healthy Planet.*

She hopes to inspire you with stories of people and their homes, educating you about what makes a green home green and how to do it—a bit at a time or all at once. Her personal mission is to empower people, especially women, in their homes and families by sharing how green and sustainability offers a safer, healthier and more comfortable home and actions to make it happen.

Acknowledgments

· · ·

THANK YOU to Brent Williams for starting our blog several years ago and teaching me the blogging habit. Thank you to all the people who have contributed to fulfilling our mission with getting meaningful, actionable green home content out in the world—Jane, Lindsey, Danielle, Krissy, and others who've touched our lives and business. From these blogs, have come this book, as well as the Green Gab Podcast, which thanks to my co-host Tony Pratte is helping to spread the word. And mostly, thank you to God and my wonderful Scott, Niki, Trent and precious family for their never-ending support.

Introduction

• • •

WELCOME. COME IN. I'd like to talk with you about green homes and why they are the very best homes of all. When you decide you want one, we'll talk about how easy it is to green your own home. And if you should win the lottery and get to choose your own dream green home, we can talk about that, too! It's all in here. Are you ready to become a green home expert? Good! Come on in!

The first home was a cave. Not the most comfortable accommodation, but caves have some definite green attributes. The temperature stays at a pretty constant level despite the weather outside. Location mattered—the sun shining on and into the opening could warm it by day, and a fire could carry on through the night. Caves provide protection from the elements and from danger in the neighborhood.

But humans being human, the search for a more comfortable home was on. They built with grass or wood or stone, and some built teepees or yurts, which had the added bonus of being transportable. But no matter what style the home or the material used to build it, the needs of the homeowners were pretty much the same: comfort and safety balanced by convenience and cost. Not much has changed (fig. 1).

FIGURE 1. What do we want in a home? Comfort, safety, and convenience that doesn't cost too much.

Well, the McMansions of the 20th century are something that cave women couldn't begin to dream of, but they are one more expression of the eternal search for a better home. In the 21st century, we see that bigger may not always be better. Our need for comfort and safety can be overwhelmed by costs—economic, physical, and social. Anyone with a castle will tell you that the heating bills will break the bank— and you're never really warm anyway. There is a better way to live like royalty in your own home (fig. 2).

FIGURE 2. Large or small, old or new, your home can be a green one, too.

When we stop to think about it, we can see how our choices in location, design, materials, and methods of heating or cooling have a direct effect on our health, our family's health, and the health of the community in which we live. Never before have we been so aware of the powerful effects of even the simple home improvement choices we make—from light bulbs to paint, roof shingles to lawns.

"What's the use of a fine house if you haven't got a tolerable planet to put it on?"

—HENRY DAVID THOREAU, *Familiar Letters*

Since the beginning, we humans have depended on the world around us to keep us alive with sunlight, food, and water (fig. 3). We still do. In spite of our ability to close the door and turn on the AC, we are still part of the natural system that creates, sustains, and perpetuates this living Earth. If, by our choices, we introduce terrible poisons into that system or waste a resource such as trees or oil that can't be renewed, we are damaging the system that includes us and the whole Earth. How do you pay back withdrawals like that? Isn't it time to look more closely at the systems in our homes and see whether they are truly serving our needs and the needs of our Earth? There are better ways to get things done.

FIGURE 3. We depend on the Earth for sunlight, food, and water.

Now, "going green" is a movement that has been kicking around for several decades, but most people think it's just about energy. It's not. It's about living healthier, more comfortable lives. And it's about having more time to go out and enjoy the world because you have already taken care of your home.

My grandmother was a young adult in the lean and challenging years of the Great Depression. She always said, "Use it up, wear it out, make it do, or do without." We're nearly 100 years from those trying times, but that still seems like the best way to live.

The whole idea of green (my point of view here) is taking responsibility for my own actions and living my values to support life in all the ways I can. That means making wise improvements on my home, driving a gas-efficient car, recycling (yes, I sometimes take it home if I can't find a recycling spot), and just turning stuff off (lights, fans, water) when I don't need them. It doesn't feel right for me to tell you about all the things we can do and not do them myself. I also recognize that I can't do everything at once, so I just make whatever changes I can today. I do something Earth friendly every day (See **Start Greening Today** box).

My mission and my passion revolve around three things: green sustainable practices, homes, and empowering women. My goal is to share my philosophy—why I want every home to be green—and my knowledge to empower women (and men) to create safer, healthier, more comfortable homes for themselves and their families. Is there anything more important than this in our lives? My responsibility to you is to share what I have learned, which is the motivation for this book, my speaking, workshops, blog, and Green Gab podcast. This information and our services are available to help you get going—whether you want to make a few better (that is, greener) choices on your next shopping trip or to build a whole new certified green home, or to accomplish something in between.

Surprisingly, it does not cost any more (and often less) to include these practices and buying habits in your daily life. Like anything else we do with a long-term payoff, it takes a little research, a little planning, and above all else, taking action. You can have the best green house in the world, but your behaviors can bring it all down. Living green has to be a blend of the stuff you buy and the things you do. If each of us built five simple practices or changes in buying habits into our daily routines, we would all soon have our own Everyday Green Home—and we would change the world.

START GREENING TODAY

Here are a few practices to start right now!

- Take out old incandescent light bulbs and put LEDs in right now. You will throw away the light bulb regardless, and the energy you save will pay for the new bulb in months.

- Turn stuff off when you aren't using it—lights, water, appliances, TV, computer. Lights are pretty easy to turn off, but do you leave the water running while you wash dishes or brush your teeth? Do you know how much water is used in producing electricity?

- Close the blinds, shades, or curtains when it is hot and sunny to keep your house cooler. In the winter, open them during the day so the sun can warm up the room.

CHAPTER ONE

What IS an Everyday Green Home?

• • •

IT'S JUST PLAIN OLD COMMON SENSE: You want your home to look great, feel great, and perform great. An Everyday Green Home is about much more than just energy and cost savings, it impacts your daily life in all of these ways:

- *Health and Safety*—breathe easier and feel healthier by reducing pollutants, toxins (chemicals, mold/mildew), and water damage through better airflow systems and quality material choices.

- *Comfort*—feel comfortable without hot/cold spots or drafts by providing a well-sealed and insulated shell and better heating, ventilating, and air conditioning (HVAC) systems.

- *Ease, Convenience, and Time*—save time by using materials, fixtures, and finishes that perform better, last longer, and require less maintenance.

- *Money*—enjoy savings in your green home with dramatically lower operating costs (especially energy) and maintenance costs. Enjoy higher selling prices for green certified homes, too.

Comfort may be the one thing that all humans are looking for in a home. Like many things in life, comfort means something different to each of us. For me comfort is an even temperature with no drafts and a hot shower (my hands and feet seem to be cold a lot). What's your definition of "all the comforts of home?" My primary goal in writing this book is to help you improve your comfort, health, and safety in your own home sweet home.

Are green homes worth more?

Yes. The home industry is on the crest of a transformational wave as we move into a "green as mainstream" world. This wave is impacting everything we know about homes, including remodeling, building new homes, and buying and selling homes.

- *Single family homes:* Currently 19% of construction projects are dedicated to including at least 90% green materials; by 2018 over 38% will be.

- *Single homebuyers:* 73% (and 68% of Multi buyers) will pay more for a green home.

- *Green homebuyers:* Represent 26–33% of the total market

As The Green Home Coach, I work with homeowners and homebuilding professionals to include green choices that have a positive impact on the world we live in together.

A Bit of BS (Building Science, That Is)

A few months ago, I spent two days in an advanced green-building class. As much as I've already learned about building science, this class gave me a glimpse of the rest of the iceberg. More importantly, it made me realize how overwhelming it can be for a homeowner to keep up with the latest developments in home improvements. It's just common sense to want our homes to be in the very best condition possible and working for us, instead of us working for them. But the complexity of the materials, systems, and components in our homes makes this very challenging. What's a homeowner to do?

We rely on our homes for many things, but especially for shelter and comfort. The numerous home systems working together to provide these comforts are often taken for granted. When you are hot or cold, the heating and cooling system jumps into action when you adjust the thermostat. If it is raining outside, the roof, siding, gutters, and windows keep you dry and comfortable (fig. 1.1). And when you return home after a long day at work, you push a button, and the garage door opens. The motion-sensor light over the front door turns on. These are all examples of the systems in our homes.

Building science is the study of how these systems affect each other. For example, airflow affects how much moisture there is in a home, which in turn can affect the growth of rot or mold. What affects airflow in your home? You might guess, "Exhaust fans in bathrooms

FIGURE 1.1. We rely on the system of roof, siding, gutters, and windows to keep us dry and comfortable.

and kitchen?" Good. Also opening a window! The HVAC system should bring in outdoor air, too. Okay, and where does moisture come from? Bathrooms, of course. But moisture also comes from cooking and drying clothes and even from breathing. Rain soaks the exterior of our house and is met by the walls, roof, and gutters. Did rain get inside somewhere? Something as simple as the choice of wall covering can affect the ability of a wall to dry out after a heavy rainstorm. Unless we're looking at things as part of interacting systems, all we know is that there is a problem with the wall and it might be water. We can't figure out where water could possibly come from in that spot (hint: it may be coming from inside the wall—not intuitive, I know.)

So back to the question, "What's a homeowner to do?" Get professional advice when you have a problem, especially when it concerns your health and safety (especially for water issues). Professionals are qualified to assess the problem and figure out ways to correct or mitigate it. I am a firm believer in getting several opinions, since everyone's experience is different, and we all handle things differently. Your least costly option—doing it yourself—may not be the best. You can search the internet for advice from experts advising homeowners with problems like yours.

Our homes are wonderful places, because they are complicated ones. We're always trying to improve on that original cave dwelling. Renovation—especially of older homes—requires really understanding building science and the way things relate to each other. For instance, caulking all of the joints and openings is a great way to air seal a home—new or existing—and contributes daily to the comfort of the residents. However, with a tighter home, the indoor air quality will be affected by any airborne chemicals released from paint, adhesives, carpets, etc. I recently experienced this in a place that was advertised as energy efficient (and it seemed to be) yet it had a slight odor and gave me headaches and body aches (fig. 1.2). This was the opposite of healthier and more comfortable.

FIGURE 1.2. Modern houses may be well-sealed, but they will make you sick if they don't have good ventilation, too.

It is likely that the builder did not pay attention to the "hidden V" in HVAC—Heating, Ventilation, and Air Conditioning. Good ventilation is critical to our health and comfort but is often overlooked by heating and cooling professionals. The HVAC system should bring in fresh air from outside throughout the day and night, or we have a problem. Several problems, in fact. We get sick, and we have moisture building up inside the home, too. Are you beginning to get a feel for how the systems interact?

The more I talk with homeowners and residents, the more I realize how much you really do want to improve your living space. On the other hand, I keep hearing from builders and members of the home industry that homeowners and residents "just don't get it." I want to be part of the solution by providing a communication link between the home industry—builders, architects, manufacturers—and us—consumers, homeowners, and residents. We know what we want or need to do in our homes **and** the home industry knows so many ways to do those jobs. Part of the conundrum has been how to illustrate basic BS (building science) in a way that homeowners and residents can digest.

How Well Does Your Home Perform?

Most of us think our home performs pretty well, at least until we add up all the utility bills. (Don't forget the water, sewer, and trash bill—they count, too!) It is so easy to forget that our homes are systems and changing one thing will impact others—the domino effect, if you will. Home Performance focuses on improving dwellings—improving comfort and health and finding ways to quit wasting money on energy and water that you don't even use. Energy systems, equipment, and appliances will continue to improve so they use less and less energy. That's for the future. In most existing homes, wasted energy continues to be a big deal, and it is impacting your wallet as well. That's exactly the point of energy efficiency: To stop wasting energy and money.

To begin to learn more about what needs improvement in your home try a quick homeowner questionnaire, "The Home Performance Challenge" at **www.BPIHomeowner.org**, a product of The Building Performance Institute, Inc. According to BPI, home performance is defined in terms of:

Comfort—a comfortable home is free of drafts, difficult temperatures, and moisture issues.

Health—a healthy home supports the health and safety of the whole family.

Efficiency—an energy-efficient home helps you stop wasting energy and money every month.

With your answers to the following questions, BPI can give you an estimate of where the energy goes and of possible energy drains in your house:

- street and zip code
- square footage of your house
- age of the house
- type of energy used to heat the house
- type of energy used to heat water

BPI then provides a graph of the probable monthly costs of heating and cooling your house, which you can adjust to show actual costs. They list improvements—which are common to every house everywhere—with the greatest cost savings first. They can put a dollar amount on those savings for you, too. Start at the top of this list, and work your way down.

- new insulation and air sealing
- new heating
- new water heating
- windows
- lighting
- cooling

The U.S. Department of Energy, at **www.EnergyStar.gov**, also provides a Home Energy Yardstick, using the same information plus the cost of 12 months of power and electricity.

Professional Home Energy Assessment

To learn more about why your house isn't comfortable or costs too much to heat, you can hire a professional. Independent (because they do not promote any products) home energy assessors ask questions about your home, and use thermal cameras to see hot and cold spots—the magic eyes into the building envelope. Homeowners that have remodeled without an energy audit often end up redoing the work to address issues that were left unresolved. Especially if your contractor does not know building science, does not understand what the problem is or know how to fix it.

Kellye Markowski, an independent energy auditor in St. Louis, says when she does a full energy audit, she is there all day investigating. She asks questions about the health and comfort of the residents and then, looks for contributing factors. Homeowners assume that their houses are built to a certain standard. Kellye has seen a lot of structures and a lot of problems. Traditional homes do not have holes sealed, or gaps between materials filled, and are often leaky. Even if you have a new home, you cannot assume that the insulation has been done correctly. In one new home, she inspected the attic to find that the one cold bedroom had no insulation at all over it. In another, the owner complained a spot was hot in summer and cold in winter. When she pushed away insulation in the attic, she found a 3-foot square hole that went all the way down through the wall to the basement. It was a simple fix to block the hole.

One client had a new heating system installed, and called her in when it didn't work as advertised. Had Kellye been in on the front end, she would have advised the ducts be handled differently. She educates homeowners and helps them compare options with all the pros and cons. When she recommends a plan of action, there is far less aggravation in working the plan.

If you're looking for an energy auditor in your area, check the Home Performance with Energy Star (HPwES) program at **www.Energy.gov**. The contractors on the list are verified by local sponsors, such as utilities, so you can be pretty confident of getting an accurate diagnosis of your home's energy, health, and comfort problems.

A Green Home Is Not All or Nothing: Making Good Decisions

Builders of new homes are already focused on energy efficiency and sustainable materials. For them, green is quickly becoming the new normal (see *Habitat for Humanity* box). But when your home is not new, you may think your green home options are limited. Not so! Each step you take can add comfort, health, and value to your home. This book can help you make smart choices and show you what to document along the way to support the value of the improvements you've made.

While you may only have a do-it-yourself project or minor replacement or upgrade, you can still use the guiding principles of green certification (see pages 120–122) to help you make buying decisions. As you will see over and over again, improvements in one area of the home will affect other areas, too. For example, new double pane windows will increase your comfort inside the house, improve the appearance and the resale value of the house, and lower your heating and AC bills, too. Win-win-win! Your home is a system of systems just like your body, and they all work together.

HABITAT FOR HUMANITY: BUILDING GREEN HOMES

Habitat for Humanity helps many people have a home of their own. To date, Habitat for Humanity of St Charles County (Missouri) has built 75 homes, all to green building principles. Michelle Woods of Habitat for Humanity of St. Charles County says, "Green Building is common sense building." The vision of Habitat for Humanity International is "a world where everyone has a decent place to live." Using green building techniques allows Habitat to build affordable homes, yet affordable does not necessarily mean cheap. It means smart and sustainable, and less expensive to operate and maintain.

There are six components that define what makes a green home green.

- Lot and site and building components
- Resource efficiency
- Energy efficiency
- Water efficiency
- Indoor air quality
- Homeowner education and documentation

These components appear throughout this book to add to your appreciation for and understanding of your own home. For example, the site and orientation of your home will have an impact on, among other things, your choice of windows, window coverings, types of lighting, and the plants you place outside those windows (fig. 1.3).

You are very blessed, indeed, if you get to choose the lot and the site and the design of a new green home. That's only a daydream for most of us who are dealing with where our home already is. But walking around your existing home can open your eyes to things that are affecting your comfort and safety and energy efficiency. Which direction does your house face? Are there lots of windows on the south side of the house bringing in heat and sunlight? Are there trees nearby that provide a windbreak in the winter or shade in the summer? Is your house on top of a hill or snuggled into a south-facing valley? How much does the wind blow in your area? Is your house in a city or a suburb or out in the woods all by itself? Is there a lot of asphalt paving around it? Is there water on your property? What kind of water? Is the soil made of sand or clay? Your answers provide you with information about the natural resources—sun, wind, rain, and soil—that have an impact on your house and on you. This is the beginning of homeowner wisdom.

FIGURE 1.3. Which way do your windows face: North, south, east, or west?

Now, take a look at the materials your house is made of—roof to walls to windows to floor. All the materials in your house have a direct impact on your comfort and health and safety—and on how much energy you use.

I've never talked to anyone that wants a home that is uncomfortable, unhealthy, and unsafe. Often, as consumers, we just assume that what we are buying will meet our expectations. Don't do that! Ask questions and have a conversation about what you expect. Comfort, health, and safety are most important in our homes, and we deserve to know how our expectations will be met when we are repairing, updating, or building a home. In a renovation or building a new home, building science professionals can help put together an optimal plan to meet your priorities, needs, and preferences. If you are just replacing light fixtures or another small job, ask for help at the hardware store—of someone who knows his/her subject. In all cases, you don't have to just buy whatever is presented to you—ask questions and do research to find out whether it's what you really want.

Water Plays a Starring Role in a Green Home

In St. Louis, Mo., we don't think about water much, because water is everywhere. But in most of the world, water is precious. Every day more than one billion people do not have clean water to drink. The most important thing about water is that all living beings need it to survive. We humans can't last a week without water, but we can go a month without food.

There is a fixed amount of water on the Earth, and it's constantly moving from one place to another in a process called the water cycle—water evaporates and rises, blown by the wind it condenses into clouds, and falls to the earth again as rain. The water that existed millions of years ago is still here today. Wherever it travels, water carries chemicals, minerals, and nutrients with it.

Fresh water is a limited but renewable resource. This means that while we can't make any more of it, we can make it safe enough to drink again. But the world's supply of clean, fresh water is decreasing. In many parts of the world, the demand for clean water exceeds the amount available, and demand continues to rise as global population grows.

So, after the air we breathe, water is our most important resource. We share it, and we all need to take care of it by not wasting it and by being careful about what goes into the sink and down the drain (fig. 1.4).

FIGURE 1.4. We share the limited amount of water on the Earth with all living beings.

The Connection Between Water Use and Energy

I am sure every parent has said it more times than they can count, "Turn off the water!" This is an important habit to instill in children, but wasting water is something that we adults need to be more aware of, too. This is about much more than turning off the faucet. Water plays a bigger role in our modern lives than most of us realize.

According to the Environmental Protection Agency's WaterSense Program (**www3.epa.gov/watersense**), a family of four in the United States uses more than 400 gallons of water each day for things like drinking, cooking, cleaning, and hygiene (fig. 1.5). That's a staggering amount of water—just imagine having to carry that much water to your house before you could use it!

FIGURE 1.5. One of the greatest comforts of home is a hot shower.

Unfortunately, leaks account for more than 13% (52 gallons for the family of four) of the water used indoors according to the Environmental Protection Agency's WaterSense program. A toilet that doesn't shut off properly and even very small leaks can result in a noticeable increase in water use. If you see an unexpected rise in your water bill, look at all the parts of your home's water system. You may need help inspecting the sprinkler system or pipes that run in areas you cannot easily access—but you definitely need to find the leak and stop it.

A family of four also uses 1,200 gallons of water every day in electricity, so that comes to a total of 1,600 gallons of water every day. What? Yes, thousands of gallons of water are used by power plants to cool and clean, key activities in making electricity. A 60-watt incandescent light bulb uses between 3,000 and 6,000 gallons of water in energy that it needs to shine 12 hours a day over the course of a year, according to a study by researchers at Virginia Polytechnic Institute and State University. Furthermore, electricity is used to clean, heat, and move water to our sinks and showers. The interdependency between energy and water is a fact. Save water by saving energy. Save energy by saving water. For more information and great graphics, go to The Union of Concerned Scientists at **www.ucsusa.org**.

Most of the electricity we use today comes from power plants burning a fuel like coal (or trash, yay!) or from nuclear power. These processes use enormous amounts of water, which is then released, still warm, into local rivers. Newer forms of creating electricity such as solar and wind use little or no water.

Almost everything we use in our daily lives has both an energy and a water cost. We just don't think about it since things aren't labeled with how much energy and water are used in their creation. Maybe they should be. There are many things you can do to save water or to use it more wisely.

- Take short showers (5 minutes).
- Turn off the tap when brushing your teeth or shaving.
- Use low-flow showerheads and faucets (fig. 1.6).
- Use the half flush button instead of full flush.
- Turn off taps snugly after using them.
- Keep drinking water in the fridge, so you don't have to wait for it to cool from the tap.
- When washing dishes, rinse them all at the end instead of each dish individually.
- Do something about leaking taps and pipes—today!
- Water the garden only when plants really need it.
- Water the roots and soil around plants rather than spraying the leaves and flowers.

- Use soaker hoses instead of sprinklers.
- Water the garden early in the morning (before 10 a.m.) or in the evening (after 4 p.m.) because less water evaporates when the air is cooler.
- Use a trigger nozzle you can turn off (or a watering can) instead of a running hose or sprinkler.
- Use a broom and not a hose (or blower) to clean paths and driveways.
- Put a rain barrel under the downspout. You can use this water to wash the car or to water flowers (not veggies because it picks up contaminants on the roof).

FIGURE 1.6. A low flow faucet looks just as stylish as any other.

"Start where you are. Use what you have. Do what you can."

—ARTHUR ASHE

CHAPTER TWO

Your Comfort, Health, and Safety: Start Where You Live

• • •

BETWEEN YOU AND THE OUTDOORS are roof, walls, windows, floors, and doors. These keep you safe and warm and comfortable inside your house. Hopefully. The roof and gutters handle the rain and snow and keep you dry. Hopefully. Inside the walls and under the roof and in the basement ceiling is insulation. Insulation acts as a sweater for your home, keeping out the wind and keeping in the heated air in the winter and the cooled air in the summer. Hopefully.

Comfort: What is a Building Envelope?

Your house, no matter what materials it is made of, surrounds you with an envelope of protection from the elements (fig 2.1). We cut into that envelope to make doors and windows, breaking the seal and letting the weather in, but there are other places where the elements can get in and where the energy you're paying for can get out. The loss of heating and cooling through these various openings costs you

FIGURE 2.1. There are so many openings in the building envelope of this little house—some you see and some you don't unless you go looking for them.

money and makes you uncomfortably cold in the winter and too hot in the summer. That is why you want to focus on sealing and insulating the envelope of your house as well as you can. This is number one on every smart homeowner's list.

I live in a three-story town-home that is almost 25 years old. It has older metal windows that are pretty leaky. I discovered a few years ago during the polar vortex that they can get really cold—and icy. The following year, I decided to get ahead of the game and winterize my windows, so I could be more comfortable. Good thing I did, too, we got our first snow just a few days later!

To weatherize the windows I purchased the window film insulation kits that I've been seeing in big box hardware stores. I ended up buying both a heavy duty and the regular version simply because of the size of my windows. They were really easy to install; I just followed the instructions. Once you tape the window film to the windows, blow it dry with a hairdryer for a little while to get the film stretched tight.

A few days after I covered the windows in my family room, temperatures plummeted to the teens—unheard of for St. Louis in November! I have to admit that my family room was much more comfortable with the window film installed. There were far fewer drafts and the amount of cold coming off my windows was dramatically reduced. In the morning when I raised my insulated blinds, I no longer felt a whoosh of cold air like I did the previous year.

The biggest expense for homeowners during the winter months is the cost of keeping warm—and that cost is expected to continue to rise. Regardless of how you heat your home, your goal should be to keep the warm air in and the cold air out.

Finding Air Leaks in Your Home

Before you can solve the problem of air leaks, you need to find them. You can hire a professional to perform an energy audit on your home. Using technology such as blower door testing and good old-fashioned know how, these home experts can quickly identify areas of your home that are allowing warm air to escape. You would be surprised at the number of little cracks that need to be sealed.

But hiring a home energy professional is not an option for everyone. One do-it-yourself method is to use smoke from a stick of incense or a candle to find areas where air is passing through exterior walls. If the smoke moves as you hold it near a closed window or door, or in front of an electrical outlet, that's a pretty good indicator of an air leak. Just be sure to take precautions not to catch the curtains on fire in the process.

The most common areas where leaks lurk in your home are:

- Windows
- Doorways
- Electrical outlets
- Attic doors and access points
- Utility entrance points

Once you have identified where the air leaks are, in most cases, it is pretty easy to seal them. A trip to the hardware or home improvement store and some time spent plugging the leaks can cut down on drafts and improve your comfort and save on heating bills over the course of the winter—and air conditioning bills in the summer.

Windows. If you are already remodeling, you might consider replacing your windows with energy-efficient ones—although the return on investment takes a while. Simply caulking around the outside and inside of the window frame can make a big difference. Also, window-sealing kits or insulated fitted blinds can add a layer of insulating air and reduce the leakage from older windows.

Doorways. Taking time to install or replace the foam rubber weather stripping along the sides and top of a doorway can seamlessly reduce and prevent airflow (fig. 2.2a and b). Replace the seal along the threshold to stop warm air from escaping and add a door sweep at the bottom of the door. (fig. 2.3) If you want to replace a door, look for the Energy Star rating. Sliding glass doors are difficult to seal—heavy drapes may be required and tinted film on the glass.

Electrical outlets. You might be surprised at how drafty electrical outlets can be. But with some easy to install outlet gaskets, you can quickly reduce air from passing through these energy-stealing openings in your walls.

FIGURES 2.2 A AND B. Foam weather stripping blocks any drafts that would come in around the door.

FIGURE 2.3. A door sweep completes the seal and helps keep an entry door draft free.

Attic accesses. Most homes have an attic access panel. While you may have plenty of insulation in the attic itself, the opening is usually not sealed well. Install a gasket or weather stripping around the inside of the opening. Also, you can glue insulation to the back of the panel to seal the whole deal. There are insulated attic covers available, too.

Utility entrance points. Electrical lines, air conditioner systems, natural gas pipes, and cables for TV all have to enter the house from the outside. They usually come in through an opening just above the foundation of the house. Take a look around the outside of your home to see if there are gaps around these entrance points. Seal them up with foam to prevent airflow.

Also seal the air ducts, which channel the heated air, and be sure they are insulated in unheated areas like crawl spaces and the attic. When all the leaks are sealed, look at putting insulation into the walls and the attic.

If you are paying for heating and cooling, you need insulation. If there already is insulation, you might need more or you may need to replace it, especially if it has gotten wet from one of the openings that you just sealed. With these two steps, you will make your home snug and warmer than before. You'll be more comfortable year round, because with the leaks plugged and insulation in all the right places, the expensive heated and air-conditioned air will stay inside your home where it belongs.

Health and Safety: Breathe Well

While plugging up drafts makes sense in terms of your comfort and health, the quality of the air in your home may not be what you think of next. But in a system, this is how one thing leads to another. With the building envelope sealed up tight, the air in your house doesn't get exchanged for fresh air unless you make it happen. Most people can't see or smell problems in air quality. They just get used to it. Irritability, low energy, aching muscles, and fatigue can all be tied to the quality of the air you breathe. Coughing, sneezing, and headaches are also signs of contaminated air. When these exposures are continued over years, chronic breathing issues, such as asthma can result. To protect your health, your home must have good ventilation.

Indoor air quality is an issue in all homes—existing or new—and all of us can improve the air we breathe. Look at when and how your home was built. Older homes were originally designed to use coal heat and are likely to be leaky on purpose. Homes from the 1970s and 1980s may be airtight but are not well ventilated.

Indoor air quality can only be improved through fresh air ventilation (remember the V in HVAC is for ventilation). You could just open the windows every night as you sleep, and turn on the whole house fan if you have one, but most people don't open the windows, especially in summer and winter. You may not have a window in your bathroom. All of this is why your heating and air conditioning system must ventilate, too. It is the lungs of your house. Other things determine what's in the air, things like mold, dust, and chemicals. You need to become more aware of the contaminants that you might be bringing in. Even just breathing inside a well-sealed house adds moisture and contaminants to the air.

How to Improve the Indoor Air Quality in Your Home

Using exhaust fans in your kitchen and baths and venting the clothes dryer to the outside are important steps, because they move the air and prevent moisture buildup that leads to mold, which is very bad for breathing. If you smoke, it's better to smoke outside. The contaminants in secondhand smoke are damaging to every member of the household, and the nicotine deposits build up in yellow layers on walls, ceiling, and furniture.

One of the easiest things you can do is to bring in plants to clean the air and provide you with oxygen. The plants breathe in the carbon dioxide that we breathe out, and give us back oxygen, fresh from the factory. Literally, the greener your home, the sweeter the air that you breathe!

Indoor Air Cleaning Systems for Your Home

Air cleaning and purifying systems are relatively new technologies to help clean the air in our homes. Systems range from using HEPA-rated air filters for your HVAC system (a fairly simple and lower cost option) to installing ionizing and UVG lamp systems (more complicated and costly). While for many of us, a HEPA filter is adequate, ionizing and UVG lamp systems may be considerations if someone in your family has asthma or another breathing condition, which require higher levels of home air purification.

You can see how the filters in your HVAC unit, which take dust and contaminates out of the air as it is drawn into the system, play an important role in the air quality in your home. Remember to change the filters often—at least every three months, but in winter when you're indoors so much, it's probably better to change them monthly. Check them more often if you have severe allergies.

Air purifiers can also help clean the air in your home. There are different types. Most use a HEPA filter that can be washed or cleaned. You can get freestanding units that plug in like a fan, and use them

TIPS FOR IMPROVING THE
AIR QUALITY IN YOUR HOME

1. **Look at updating your HVAC system with an air cleaning system.** Have the system checked yearly and change the filters at least every three months. Ask the HVAC technician about increasing the number of air exchanges of the HVAC system (so it "breathes" more often.)

2. **Control pollutants coming in as much as possible.** Choose less-toxic or non-toxic paint, adhesives, sealants, caulk, flooring, wall coverings, cabinetry, and furnishings. Look for materials without urea formaldehyde. Volatile organic chemicals (VOCs) off-gas and contribute to poor indoor air quality. Low- to no-VOC paints, finishes, sealants, and adhesives are easy to find and offer great performance with fewer toxins. Check the GreenGuard (**www.greenguard.org**) and Green Seal (**www.greenseal.org**) websites for recommended choices. If you can't find a low-VOC product for the job you're doing, you can remove some of the chemicals in the air by opening the windows for a few days, but realize that the chemicals can continue to off-gas for a long time. Pesticides, paints, adhesives, and solvents should only be used in well-ventilated areas. Open windows and doors when using them and try to use them only when no one else is at home.

3. **Seal off the air from an attached garage to keep fumes and exhaust out.** Weather stripping or adding a gasket around the door to the garage helps in both new and existing homes. If you have a fireplace, be sure it is vented correctly. Seek professional help with this.

4. **Store chemicals safely, or better yet, limit use of chemicals in your home and yard.** Many household and yard products contain toxic chemicals and fumes. If the product is hazardous to children and pets, do you want to have it around at all? There are good non-toxic choices.

5. **Look for roof leaks and replace water-stained ceiling tiles and carpeting.** Mold grows happily in these places. Find out how your attic is ventilated, and make sure it is working properly.

6. **Vacuum often with a HEPA filter vacuum cleaner.** Dust often with microfiber cloths.

7. **Bring in plants** to clean the air and provide you with oxygen.

where you need them most, but it may be more efficient and effective to get a filter that is made to be part of your home heating and cooling system. Check with your local HVAC professional. He can also give you advice on duct cleaning, which can make a big difference because dust and contaminates settle in the ducting of the system as well.

Doing the Research for You

It can be overwhelming just to try to think of all the products you buy to use in your home—how will you ever find time to figure out which ones are environmentally friendly and non-toxic and the ones you want to use? Fortunately, there are non-profit organizations that set standards, inspect, and certify thousands of products to assure you (and your builder) that they are produced in and perform in sustainable, renewable, and environmentally friendly ways (see **Resources** on page 133). The organizations identify what's in stuff and what is considered safe enough to be in our homes. When it comes to air quality, look for the Green Seal checkmark or the GreenGuard logo.

At Green Seal's website (**www.greenseal.org**), you find information on household products, construction materials, paints, printing and writing paper, household paper products (e.g., towels, napkins), food packaging, hand soap and cleaners, cleaning services, and personal care products.

UL Environment's GreenGuard Certification program (**www.greenguard. org**) helps manufacturers create—and helps buyers identify and trust—products and materials with low chemical emissions, improving the quality of the air where the products are used. The GreenGuard Product Guide is an online tool for finding certified low-emitting products for offices, hospitals, schools, and homes.

What Does Cleaning Have to Do With Air Quality?

One of the most important parts of cleaning is removing dust from your home. Despite your best efforts, dust always settles back on surfaces all over the house. A big part of the dust in a home is actually dead skin cells from humans and pets. (I know, sounds gross, but this is a fact of life.) It tends to accumulate faster during the winter months, because we spend a lot more time indoors. Add the fact that winter also means lower humidity drying out our skin, and before you know it, you can write your name on any flat surface.

The amount of dust in your home has a major impact on the quality of the air for you and your family. And if dusting is not done correctly, you may actually make it worse rather than better. Traditional methods of cleaning, such as dusting spray and feather dusters, can actually lead to more dust and more work for you. Using aerosol sprays that promise a shiny, protected surface often leave an oily film behind. While this may make the wood in your home appear to be clean, the film attracts dust. When this happens, guess what? You have to work harder to remove the dust next time and dirt can become trapped between layers of oily film.

A feather duster may remove dust initially but causes it to become airborne. When dust goes into the air, it can take up to eight hours to settle to the ground or on other surfaces. While it is suspended in the air, you and your family are breathing it. Yucky! Additionally, when it does finally settle, you are right back where you started.

The Correct Methods for Dusting Your Home

The best dusting methods remove the dust. Vacuum cleaners are the most effective method of removing dust, because carpeting is the biggest air filter in your home, collecting all that settling dust. For above the floor dust, use the vacuum cleaner attachments to remove as much dust as you can. Make sure to replace the vacuum filter often and to empty the bag or container even more often. This prevents the dust from being returned to the air.

When vacuuming isn't an option, microfiber cleaning tools are very effective at grabbing the soil and holding on to it. Microfiber works so well, because it is constructed of synthetic fibers that contain little chambers that hold the dirt rather than push it along. It is possible to collect and remove even microscopic particles from all sorts of places (see **Spring Cleaning** box). Microfiber works well dry, but to make it even more effective, mist a tiny amount of water directly onto the microfiber itself. You don't want to apply water to wooden furniture but using a minimal amount of tap water will help remove a lot of dust. The best part is that most microfiber cleaning tools are washable. (And most commercial dusting sprays have chemicals you don't want in your house, anyway.) All of this saves you breath and money!

SPRING CLEANING:
DON'T FORGET TO DUST HERE!

Light fixtures and bulbs. Light bulbs last longer when dusted regularly.

Vent covers. Air intake and room HVAC vents collect a lot of dust. Also, don't forget the exhaust fan vents in your bathrooms, too!

Furniture structures and supports. Reclining chairs and pull-out sofas have lots of hardware under them where dust settles. Reach under or flip them over and wipe down the supports and mechanisms.

Inside cabinets and closets. Because we rarely remove all of the contents from cabinets, spring cleaning is a good time to take the opportunity to clean out the cabinets and closets where dust loves to hide!

Blinds and other window treatments. There are several microfiber cleaning tools on the market that make cleaning blinds much easier. For curtains and other window treatments, many professional laundry services run specials in the spring on cleaning delicates such as curtains. Some will even take down the dirty ones for you and replace them after cleaning.

Ceiling fans. It is always surprising to see the amount of dust that ceiling fans collect. Pull out a stepstool or a ladder and wipe them down!

It is also important to give pets a bath on a regular basis to minimize exposure to dander. Most people don't realize how difficult it is to remove the microscopic dead skin cells that make up pet dander from upholstery and carpet.

Chemicals in the Air: What's That I Smell?

Many cleaning products contain strong chemicals and synthetic fragrances that have been found to be damaging to our health—especially when we're breathing them in an enclosed environment (and, worse, sending them down the drain into our water supply). Too many of these chemicals also cause genetic changes and cancer. It's wiser and healthier and cheaper to use the same cleaning solutions our grandmothers did—baking soda and white vinegar. A diluted solution of vinegar and water will kill the germs in your kitchen and bath. (It is interesting to note that scientists now say our immune systems need germs to work properly, so buying products that destroy any and all microscopic life seems not to be the best thing for our health after all.)

Synthetic fragrances hide in many products, especially those for laundry and personal care, but, ironically, those made to "freshen" the air are just as bad for you to breathe—even scented candles are a problem. Add to the baddie list oven cleaners, tarnish and mold removers, and most counter and floor cleaning solutions. Check out the Environmental Working Group's Cleaners Hall of Shame (**www.ewg.org/guides/cleaners**) for more details. Hair care products are another place that fragrances play a big role and are bad for you to breathe. When you see "fragrance" or "parfum" in the ingredients of a product, it means there are harmful chemicals in the product— chemicals that you don't want to become part of you.

Air fresheners don't really freshen the air; they just add chemicals to it. Better to open the windows and let the sunshine in and the breeze blow through. You can set out a dish of baking soda or a bowl of white vinegar in a room that needs freshening. Or you can use real essential oils in an air diffuser. The herbs and flowers that the oils are made from bring fragrances directly from nature to refresh the air. As an added bonus, essential oils have been shown to improve mood and health. Different oils have different effects; for example, breathing in lavender essential oil relaxes you and breathing in grapefruit or orange essential oil invigorates you.

If you love your brand of laundry detergent or shampoo, try the unscented ones. But also try some of the products that were consciously created to be healthy. Or save money and go back to your grandmother's methods. No, not all the way back to making soap in a big iron kettle over a fire in the front yard, but just far enough back to escape the chemicals in all those brightly packaged products on grocery store shelves.

It shouldn't be surprising that nature has everything you need. You can find many useful tips online about how to go natural in cleaning yourself and your house—and improving the quality of the air that you and your family breathe.

Over the years, I've moved to cleaning with fewer and fewer chemicals. When my children were younger, they both had migraines and exhibited chemical sensitivities. I began paying attention to the chemicals I was bringing into our home, especially soaps, detergents, and cleaners. I started a quest for better ways to clean without a bunch of chemicals. There are many choices in our local grocery or big box store. Even more options are available online or at specialty stores. Or you can make your own! It turns out that vinegar, baking soda, and lemons make great cleaners and have been used for this for centuries.

For more information about making your own green cleaners, check the Homeowner Resources at Home Nav **http://my.homenav.com/resources/green-living/household-chemicals/green-cleaning.php** (you need to be logged in). Or shop online for non-toxic, healthy cleaners. Whether you are a D-I-Yer or just a buyer, there are many healthier options for cleaning your home.

Nature to the Rescue

Plants are the natural system for refreshing the air inside—and outside—your home. They take in carbon dioxide and produce oxygen. We breathe in oxygen and breathe out carbon dioxide. It's a match made in Heaven. Plants can also take contaminants out of the air. A study by NASA in the 1980s (Interior Landscape Plants for Indoor Air Pollution Abatement) produced a list of houseplants that clean the air by absorbing contaminates. This comes in handy in the extremely closed environments of spacecraft and can do the same in your home. Online you'll find websites with lists of plants identified as air cleaners, and plant nurseries may have plants tagged as "Clean Air" for easy selection. These are the plants NASA tested:

- Gerbera daisy
- English ivy
- Pot mum
- Marginata
- Peace lily

- Mother-in-law's tongue
- Warneckei
- Bamboo palm
- Mass cane
- Janet Craig
- Chinese evergreen
- Heart leaf philodendron
- Elephant ear philodendron
- Green spider plant
- Golden pothos
- Aloe vera
- Ficus

NASA put activated carbon air filters in the root area of the plants with a small fan attached and filtered more polluted air more quickly than the plants did alone. See the NASA study at **http://tinyurl.com/ gu7g8a4**.

Recently, a CEO in Delhi, India, Kamal Meattle, suffered severe headaches and breathing difficulties from the poor air quality in his office. To remove contaminants and get more oxygen circulating, he brought in lots of plants (4–8 plants in each group) to line the walls of the office and to work removing formaldehyde and volatile chemicals from the air. His breathing and physical condition improved so much it made the news! The plants he used were Areca palm, Mother-in-law's Tongue, and Money Plant (Epipremnum oureum).

You and your family spend so much time in your home. Make sure the air is as clean as you can possibly make it.

CHAPTER
THREE

Energy Efficiencies: How Can You Be Comfortable and Get the Most for Your Energy Dollars?

• • •

WHERE DO YOU START when you want to start greening your home? Looking out the windows? Walking around the outside? What is your focus? I think you must start with the thing that is affecting your own comfort right now. For example, you're cold. Some of the systems that come into play when you're cold are the building envelope, the heating and the ventilation system, the windows, the window coverings, and even the ceiling fan. This chapter is about the systems that make up your home and the resources to help you get the most out of these systems. We hope to open your eyes to a whole new way of thinking about your house.

Windows

Windows are great. They give us light, views, warmth, and ventilation (fig. 3.1)! They're also not so great, because they put big holes in the

FIGURE 3.1. Windows let in light, views, warmth, and ventilation!

middle of a wall. Knowing this when you plan to build a house, replace your windows, or just work with your existing windows, can help you use your windows to their best advantage. Your windows can be a big source of heat gain and loss as well as drafts. What do you do? How do you figure out what to do?

Since the sun is already shining on your house, you can use it for heat and light. That's called passive solar heating, and humans have been using it for thousands of years (remember the cave). So where is the sun in relation to your windows?

Site and Location

Let's look at windows from the point of view of a compass. The sun rises in the east and shines strongly into windows on that side of your house. You'll need blinds to keep out the glare, especially if this is your bedroom. You can also soak up some of the heat from this strong sunlight with a dense, dark floor. In the winter, the thermal mass of the floor will release this warmth into the air slowly over the day. In the summer, you don't want the heat collecting there, so pull down the shade! (See figure 3.2.)

FIGURE 3.2. When the summer sun is hitting your windows, pull down the shade.

The south side of your house gets sun for most of the day. Hopefully these are the rooms where you spend most of the day and get the benefit of the sunlight and warmth. For summer, you could install awnings on south-facing windows, if there is not enough overhang from the roof to provide shade for those windows. (Yes, go outside and check.) You need to consider how awnings will look on your style of architecture—usually fine on the back of the house, seldom good for the front. You can also plant trees to shade these windows or set up a trellis and train plants to grow up it. When the trees and plants drop their leaves in winter, you'll welcome the additional sunlight in those windows.

West facing windows receive the long rays of the setting sun, again resulting in glare in your eyes, so blinds or shades are important for these windows, too. Dark floors will soak up the warmth of the sun and release it into the air of your home slowly overnight.

North facing rooms have the least amount of natural light. They're always darker and colder than the rest of the house. You'll probably want the shades open to let in what little light there is, so be sure the window is well sealed and as energy efficient as you can make it. Light colors in the room may help and good electric lighting. This might be a good room for watching TV, since you don't need strong lighting to do that.

Increasing Energy Efficiency

Windows are one of the biggest causes of energy loss in a home. The least energy efficient window has a single pane of glass. If you add a second pane of glass, it's more efficient (doesn't let in as much cold); and if you put gas in-between the two pieces of glass, it's better yet. If you put a tinted film on the glass that reflects sunlight away from the window, you get an even higher energy efficiency rating. Wooden windows are better at not conducting cold air than are metal ones, but wood exposed to the elements requires more maintenance. Of course, if the weather stripping around the window is worn or missing and the holes around the window frame are not caulked, then even the best windows will still leak your heated and cooled air.

Look for the Energy Star rating. The Energy Star label means this product meets an energy-savings rating from the U.S. Environmental Protection Agency. Windows receive Energy Star ratings just like lighting and appliances do to help you decide which to choose. At

www.Energy.gov you can learn much more about windows—types of glass, frame materials, insulating gasses, tints or film, and what the energy ratings mean.

Look at your windows. If they slide to open, horizontally or vertically, they are leakier than windows that are cranked (or pushed) open and can be locked into place when closed. If your windows slide or push up, you could add storm windows on the outside to stop leaks. Storm windows provide another seal against the outside air.

When I used to think of ways to be more energy efficient, I would jump to updating the windows but, realistically, that is not always the best option. Instead of buying expensive new windows, make sure the windows are properly sealed, and start looking for new window coverings instead. Looking at window coverings with green eyes, you'll see the energy savings they can bring you in all seasons—in addition to color, design, and more comfortable temperatures inside your home.

Window Coverings

Windows are places that a lot of your air-conditioned air is lost during hot weather. By installing light-colored window shades or blinds, you can reflect sunlight back outside and reduce solar heat gain by as much as 50%. A great way to save money in both heating and cooling is to invest in good shades (fig 3.3). Shades and other window coverings aren't just for style anymore!

FIGURE 3.3. Honeycomb shades with a dual layer of cells insulate and filter light.

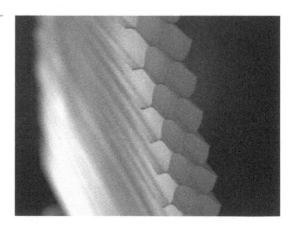

There are draperies, curtains, plantain shutters, and shades. All vary in their ability to block heat or cold depending on the style or material. The thickness of the fabric affects the amount of heat blocked. Layered window treatments of blinds, covered by curtains or drapes topped by valences provide a multi-layered and effective barrier to sunlight and cold (fig. 3.4). If you like the curtains open, try closing them just while you're at work—or have tinted film applied to the window to reflect the sunlight.

FIGURE 3.4. Layered window treatments of insulated blinds covered by curtains provide a multi-layered and effective barrier to both heat and cold.

If you prefer not to have any type of curtains on your windows, there are awnings (fig. 3.5), outdoor blinds, screens, window overhangs, or shutters that you can install on the exterior of your house to block the sun. Hanging tightly woven bamboo screens outside the window during the summer can stop more than 75% of the sun's heat from reaching your windows. For more great options visit **www.Energy.gov** for a full list of window coverings.

FIGURE 3.5. Awnings provide welcome shade on south-facing windows in the summer.

Lighting

Lighting is not just about bulbs and lamps. Lighting comes in many forms for our homes: natural sunlight, overhead lighting to brighten a room, and task lighting to read, work, or cook by. Lighting adds a wonderful decorative and mood boosting element to our homes too.

Daylighting

Let's start with daylighting. Daylight is a combination of sunlight, light diffused by the earth's atmosphere, and light reflected from the ground or other surfaces. It's all free. We want to let daylight in through windows, skylights, or sun tubes. In the world of green homes, this lighting is deliberately directed to certain areas to reduce the need for turning on electric lights. Since light naturally diffuses, certain types of surfaces and colors can help "extend" light into the room. For instance, white tiles or countertops spread available light and makes the bathroom or kitchen feel brighter. The use of high or clerestory windows will bring light deeper into a room. Skylights offer a different light pattern and a great way to bring all-over light to a room (fig. 3.6). Most of the time with a skylight you do not need additional artificial light during daylight hours. With the advanced skylights available today, you can get daylight, energy-efficiency, and ventilation all in one package.

FIGURE 3.6. A skylight lets in lots of natural light.

The best daylighting option is to open up all the windows (or all the blinds) to let the sun in during the day. Tinted film on windows protects from UV rays and still lets the light in. Types of windows that give good light are: skylights, transom windows, bay windows, clerestory windows, and picture windows.

If you have the opportunity to build a new house, you have the ability to position your building. South is the best side for bringing in light; windows are essential here. East and west facing windows receive the long rays of the sun in the morning or evening, which causes high glare in those rooms, so you don't want too many windows on those sides. Bay windows overlooking the back yard provide a great view and good light. A picture window in the kitchen or living room will bring the outdoors in. In renovations, many people brighten up a room by adding a bay or a picture window—just, please, be sure that it is well insulated and sealed, especially below the window. It needs to look good and perform well!

Ceiling Color and Light

White ceilings reflect light better than black (or dark) ceilings (fig. 3.7). White ceilings make the room appear larger while black (or dark) ceilings seem to "close in" on a person. Ceilings are difficult to paint. Once you paint them white, it is easier to change the wall color frequently without the added hassle of having to re-do the ceiling. That said, there's no rule about painting a ceiling white. If you want to try a dark ceiling, go for it! Also note that reverse shades that lower from the top of the window cast light on the ceiling, too.

FIGURE 3.7. The white ceiling reflects and diffuses the light from the fixture.

Decorating with Lights

One way to liven up your home is by upgrading your lighting. Adding a wall sconce or a few pendent lights can make a dark room come alive! You can find advice on selecting fixtures, installation tips, and Energy Star recommendations for many different types of lighting online, at big box stores, and at lighting stores. You might also be adventurous and look into adding a solar tube for some natural light as well.

I once met a woman who had just renovated a bathroom with no windows. She had gotten carried away finding a hanging lamp with blown glass shade to match the Mexican painted porcelain sink. The colors in the room were gorgeous, but the lamp, hanging next to the mirror and focused down at the sink, didn't provide nearly enough light, nor was it at the right height. Sadly, the amount she had budgeted for the renovation was all gone, and you still can't see yourself in the mirror.

Keeping Things Light

To get the most benefit from your windows, light fixtures, and lamps, you need to keep them clean. Dirty windows, dusty light fixtures/lamps, and grubby walls reduce the effectiveness of both daylight and artificial light. (Not to mention how that kind of environment makes you feel.) Dirt reduces performance on windows by 10% or more, on lamps by 20-25%. Good maintenance is essential.

So get out the white vinegar and water mixture and some old newspapers and make your windows sparkle again. Dusting with a microfiber cloth will brighten up the lamps and, for the walls? Wipe off handprints and grime and vacuum off the dust. If that doesn't work, perhaps it's time for a new coat of paint?

LEDs: Super Heroes

LEDs (light emitting diodes) are the Super Heroes of the light bulb world, small but mighty—and amazingly efficient. Since the federal government required light bulbs to become 30% more efficient by 2012, there have been huge changes, not just in the shape of light bulbs but in the way they work. LEDs have been around for many years, for example, forming the numbers on digital clocks and telling us when our appliances are turned on, but mostly we know them as way cool Christmas lights. They are so much more.

LEDs are different from other light bulbs. The biggest difference is one versus many. An incandescent light bulb has a single filament inside one glass bulb. An LED bulb is made up of many tiny diodes, and each one gives off light but very little heat (fig 3.8).

FIGURE 3.8. LEDs have many tiny lights inside the bulb.

LEDs have many benefits over conventional light bulbs. They are far more energy efficient. They don't get hot, and they last years longer, because they don't have a filament that will burn out. They are more durable than all other kinds of bulbs.

According to **www.Energy.gov**, traditional incandescent lights, conventional or halogen, are huge energy consumers, with only 10% of the energy they use being converted into light. The other 90% is emitted as heat. They also have a very short lifespan compared to other sources of lighting.

Compact fluorescent lights (CFL) are the twisted bulbs that many of us have in our lamps these days. They are more energy-efficient than incandescent bulbs, but they are not nearly as energy efficient as LEDs. Their energy consumption is approximately 20% toward creating light and 80% to heat. They have a longer life span than incandescent bulbs, (1000–3000 hours depending on the quality and type of lighting), so they really made sense when it came to alternatives to traditional bulbs. They did, until LEDs entered the picture. Also, they have an environmental cost. The chemicals in fluorescent lights (argon and mercury) are dangerous or toxic, and can contaminate landfills. They also can be slow to come on, causing frustration for users.

LED light bulbs address all of these issues. First of all, LEDs convert a lot more energy into light rather than into heat. Their conversion is 80–90% light. That is a huge difference! Instant cost savings. This in turn, also means that they are far cooler to the touch, which results in a safer product and greater comfort while you're using them. They do not need time to warm up, achieving full brightness instantly. And, they are 95% recyclable!

It's easy to see why LEDs took over Christmas lighting so quickly.

THREE TIPS FOR LED HOLIDAY LIGHTS

1. **Replace old holiday lights with new LED lights.** They last longer, burned out bulbs are easier to replace, and they use less energy.

2. **Recycle your old lights locally, or you can mail them to www.HolidayLEDs.com.** Yes, there's really a website and company that shred the lights, then sort the raw materials (pvc, glass, copper) so they can be reused.

3. **Rethink your holiday light designs with LEDs.** They use less electricity with no heat, so you can string more together without creating a safety hazard or running up a big electricity bill. You can run them on batteries (think front door wreath, candles in windows), and they come in so many colors.

The best way to demonstrate the energy savings possible with LED lights is to look at traffic lights, which are made up of rows of LEDs, each one the size of a pencil eraser. Many cities are replacing traditional halogen bulbs, which use 50–150 watts, with LED units for three reasons. The new LEDs save a lot of energy, they last for years versus traditional bulbs that only last months, and they are brighter. The LEDs are arranged to provide equal brightness across the entire surface. The energy savings will be huge. If a traffic light uses 100-watt bulbs, 24 hours a day, that equals 2.4 kilowatt-hours per day. If a kilowatt-hour costs 8 cents, a single traffic signal costs 20 cents a day or $73 per year to operate. A typical intersection has eight stoplights, so a single intersection costs roughly $600 per year. Big cities have thousands of intersections, so you can see why cities are switching to LED lights, with the potential to save millions of dollars each year.

My mother has been a hold out. She did not have good luck with some energy-efficient bulbs she tried and felt most didn't have the right color. Recently, while I was visiting her house, and she was away for the afternoon, I purchased four dimmable LED spotlights and installed them for her. These lights are great! At full brightness they are a cool white or daylight color—perfect for the room in office mode. Dim the lights down and they gradually turn to a soft warm glow—just right for TV room mode. Talk about a perfect light for a room that serves as an office during the day and a family room at night.

When my mother came back and tried the lights, she loved them. As a matter-of-fact, she loved them so much that she purchased more for other rooms in her house. Success! And better yet, these LED bulbs should not need to be changed for years—a bonus with ceiling spotlights.

As with any developing technology, the purchase price of LED light bulbs is still higher than a traditional equivalent. This is changing quickly as they become more popular and technology advances. My mother and I justify the difference in cost as well worth it since she won't have the hassle of changing bulbs in hard to reach areas again, and she's saving on her electric bill, too. You will be amazed when you compare the three types of bulbs in the LED comparison charts on the internet. For starters, LEDs last for 50,000 hours, incandescent bulbs 1,200, and CFLs 8,000.

LED bulbs have come a long way in a few short years. Not only will they save you electricity costs right off the bat (estimated yearly cost of one bulb in my dining room is 90 cents), but they last so long (22.8 years in my dining room). They come in many shapes and sizes, and I've found a wide variety in local lighting stores, as well as in big box stores, grocery stores, and online. I've had great success with them and hope you will give them a try, and see what works for you in your home.

Lighting Zones

Light switches turn your lights on, off, or dim them. You can also integrate lights into zones dedicated to an activity or mood you want to create. You can control these lighting zones with traditional light switches, a master wall panel (like a programmable thermostat), or a smart phone app. LEDs will play the starring role (fig. 3.9). Your lighting zones might include:

- *Arriving home zone*—lights on the porch and in the entryway, or the garage and kitchen if that's where you enter your house.
- *Cooking zone*—the kitchen ceiling lights and task lighting under the cabinets.
- *Kids's zone*—lights in areas designated for homework and/or playing.
- *Nighttime*—bedrooms and the bathroom.
- *Outdoor entertaining*—lights on deck/patio and walkways for guests to walk safely.
- *Away from home*—used on workdays or reserved for vacations. Randomly turn lights on and off (with timers) to make people think someone is home.

FIGURE 3.9. In zone lighting this eat-in kitchen, there are pendant lights over the counter/bar area, spotlights over the cooking area, and a chandelier over the dining table.

You can create your own automated lighting zones with a do-it-yourself starter kit. You can start with a kit that includes a wireless hub that plugs into your home's router, and several LED bulbs controlled through the hub, and add bulbs as you identify other zones you want to light.

You could hire a home automation company to install a single zone or a whole house system. This can be a large investment, so ask about other home automation systems you can get at the same time. These might include home security and raising/lowering window coverings for energy savings. I don't know about you, but I don't want any more remote controls, so the more I can get into one, the better.

Automation

The home of the Jetsons has arrived. With technology available today, the home of the future is here—a home where the lights turn on as you approach the driveway, the temperature adjusts before you get home, and the coffee maker starts on cue. There are refrigerators that let us know when we run out of milk and dishwashers that run when electricity is the least costly.

The Internet allows home systems and appliances to communicate with a controller or smart phone/tablet app. Automation allows you to pre-set schedules to take advantage of energy and cost savings while your home is not occupied or during low use or sleep times. Sensors allow systems to shift automatically to deal with changes in conditions, such as time, light, temperature, and humidity. Home automation can include an energy-tracking program to help you see where improvements are needed and savings are being accomplished. An automated home can contribute to your safety, comfort, convenience, and savings.

Home technology may be the path to a new era of safety and independence for seniors allowing them to age in place longer. Family can be notified of irregular behavior or an emergency within moments via communications and alarms. Family and friends can remotely change or control temperature and lighting while also monitoring activity and safety.

The field is growing so rapidly all we can do here is offer a few glimpses of how much exciting new technology is heading toward our homes.

- Dynamic lights can follow the natural rhythms of daylight to help those with seasonal affective disorder (SAD). These light bulbs are also called full-spectrum bulbs.

- Digital doorbells have combined doorbells with cameras, so you can answer the door via your smart phone, no matter where you are.

- Digital door locks are connected to smart phones.

Heating

Typically about half your utility bill goes to heating. So, you'll get the most bang for your buck when you upgrade for energy efficiency here. You will, that is, IF your home is well insulated and air-sealed to keep the hot air where it belongs!

Home heating is a necessity in most homes in the U.S. Certain fuels, such as natural gas or heating oil, are used in different regions of the country, depending on how convenient they are to get. Few of us try to heat our houses with fireplaces any more. Some of us have radiators that heat with steam, an old but dependable system. Most of us have a boiler, furnace, or heat pump that heats air or water, which is circulated through ducts or radiators or baseboard units. These central heating systems warm up our entire home and are a big improvement on fireplaces. (But not as pretty to look at.)

When you start thinking about selecting a heating system, you'll need to consider fuel options and the cost of each type, climate, efficiency (Energy Star), and the right size for your house. Your choices in home heating are furnaces, boilers, heat pumps, active solar, and electric. Do you want the system to cool your home as well? And provide ventilation? Are there health concerns? For example, radiant heaters don't distribute allergens as ducted systems do.

If you want to compare heating systems, look at the Energy Saver 101 infographic at **http://www.Energy.gov/articles/energy-saver-101-infographic-home-heating**. It explains the different types on the market, how they work, and what to look for when replacing your system. Before you get a new heating system, be sure to air-seal and insulate your home. With no leaks, you can meet your heating needs with a smaller sized unit, which will save on purchase cost and operating costs, too. Be sure the air ducts and heating pipes are properly sealed, too.

In Europe, where energy is more expensive, it has long been a practice to heat the room or the zones where the people are. To do this, you might use space heaters such as wood or pellet stoves, portable or direct vent wall heaters, or a fireplace that re-circulates warm air. If you use any of these, you must have a carbon monoxide detector in your house. Hot water baseboards are good for zone heating but slow to heat the whole room. Electric baseboards are quiet and low maintenance. Radiant heating uses a heated liquid running through tubes embedded in or under the floor. There is even a low voltage radiant heater that can run directly from solar panels. Radiant heaters can be used in floor, ceiling, or wall panels. If in the floor, cover it with tiles so they hold and radiate heat into the room. Radiant heat can be fueled by boiler, heat pump, active solar, and electric (see fig. 3.10). Whatever type of heating system you have, make sure air vents, baseboard heaters, and radiators are clean and free of obstructions.

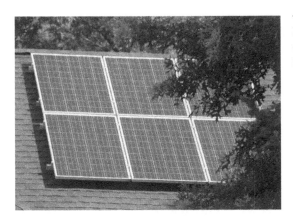

FIGURE 3.10. Solar energy can heat your home and the hot water that you use, too.

Don't forget the attic! If it is not sealed and insulated, your utility dollars can literally go through the roof. This is such a common issue in homes that most heating and cooling companies offer some variation of financial assistance to help you properly insulate your attic. Some people have their heating and cooling system in the attic, but if it is not properly insulated, the system runs inefficiently, increases your bill, and fails sooner. Unless you know your attic is fitted with an R38 measure of insulation, (which translates to about a foot), have it checked and sealed. As for the heating and cooling unit itself, tell your contractor specifics about your home and about any insulation work you have had done to be sure he/she fits your home with the right sized unit.

Air Conditioning

Picture yourself back in 1904 when the World's Fair was held in St. Louis. It's a typical St. Louis summer—hot and muggy. You can imagine sitting on your big front porch with a tall glass of iced tea, courtesy of the ice just delivered from the local iceman. Thank goodness for the icebox, iced tea, and breezy porches. Air conditioning has just been invented but there will be quite a few years before it's commonly used in houses. At first air conditioning was used in public places, making going to the movies, a popular event, much more pleasant.

In much of the Midwest, whole house fans were used to bring cool night air in the open windows and through the house and up to the attic. They're noisy, but they work. Window mounted room air conditioners appeared in homes soon after and helped with a good night's sleep on hot nights. I do recall those window units were noisy, too, when I was a little girl at my grandparents in South Texas. I'd plant myself in front of the window AC to cool off! Air conditioning, especially central air conditioning, changed how and where we can live and work. Air conditioning has made possible the vast migration to the south. Can you imagine millions of people choosing to move to Houston, Atlanta, or Phoenix without air conditioning?

Nowadays we seldom give a second thought to air conditioning—at least not as long as it's working. Ever notice how it always goes out (or the power does) on one of the hottest days of the summer? Air conditioning is a way of life for most of us these days.

Air conditioning has not only changed where we live and work, it has changed how we live and work. With the advent of air conditioning, television, and electronics, our lives have pretty much moved indoors and became private in a new sort of way. It used to be that people were always outside on the porch or working in the breeze and talking with neighbors. Even architecture changed as homes and buildings no longer needed to rely on local climate and natural ventilation to stay cool. The regional uniqueness of architecture in different climate types has all but disappeared in today's air-conditioned homes. The big porches that invited us to come and sit in the shade awhile are no longer considered necessary. (They still are necessary, by the way.)

Of course, air conditioning comes with a cost. Much of our electric bill is due to air conditioning. Expand that to public buildings, homes, and vehicles. Air conditioning places a heavy load on our electric systems, infrastructure, and fuel, especially at the hottest time of the day when peak load electricity is often needed to keep up with the demand for air conditioning. There are ways to reduce the energy demands of air conditioning at your house.

REDUCE YOUR AC LOAD WITHOUT BREAKING A SWEAT

Here are a few things you can do to stay cool and help reduce the strain on your wallet, the electricity loads, and your community.

Inside your home

- **Service your air conditioning system annually.** This preventative maintenance will keep your unit running well and head off bigger issues down the road.

- **Change your filter regularly.** Check your owners' manual (if you don't have it, you may be able to find it online) for manufacturer's recommended schedule. If in doubt, change your filter every 3 months. Besides helping your AC to run more efficiently, this helps keep your inside air cleaner.

- **Keep air supply and return vents clean** and free of obstructions to help optimize efficiency.

- **Install and use ceiling fans.** The moving air from the fan makes you feel cooler, so you can set the thermostat a little higher. Installing a fan is a beautiful decorative accent as well. When it's not too hot, use just the fan (or a freestanding fan) instead of the air conditioner.

continued on next page

continued from previous page

- **Consider a whole house fan.** It makes you whole house cooler for less than AC costs.

- **Replace light bulbs with LED bulbs.** They will reduce the load on your air conditioner (traditional incandescent bulbs create a lot of heat!)

- **Install and use window treatments.** Window treatments don't just look good, they also help control light and heat—protecting your furnishings and helping reduce your utility bills. Close curtains during the day to prevent heat and solar gain. Blinds and curtains that diffuse or direct the light are especially helpful on east and west windows to help control glare.

- **When buying a new air conditioner,** choose an energy-efficient model (check at **www.Energy.gov**) and have it sized using ACCA-certified Manual J and S software to ensure you are getting the best sized unit for your home. Be sure this large investment will be the best one for your house.

Outside your home

- **Plant trees near your home** to provide shade and keep it naturally cool.

- **Keep outside air conditioning or heat pump unit clean** and free of obstructions to help optimize efficiency.

- **Shade your outside air conditioning or heat pump unit.** You may wish to consult a professional since you do not want to obstruct the unit by planting too close, nor do you want to damage the tree or bush because those units put off quite a breeze when operating.

I got a little taste of my own medicine one day when my air conditioner went out. Luckily, it wasn't too unbearable. I had actually been sleeping with the windows open. Well, the blower motor was running so the air was coming through, but it was not cool. I figured I might as well use it as an opportunity to learn. (I was thrilled to be able to tell the repairman that, yes, I have an energy-efficient air conditioner and furnace.) Fortunately, I did not have to replace the outside unit—the compressor—but he did have to replace two of the workings of the compressor capacitor (that took me back to engineering classes) and the band motor. As he worked, he explained how these parts get less efficient with age and affect the efficiency of the entire system. This was something I honestly had not given much thought to. Even with a high-efficiency air conditioning system, I was not getting all the benefits, because some parts were worn out. This was a good reminder of how important it is to keep up with routine maintenance, so the energy efficiency you start with continues to serve you well.

Thermostats: Controlling Your Comfort Level

Should You Set Back Your Thermostat?

One topic that seems to get a lot of back and forth (pun intended) is "Should you set back your thermostat to conserve energy?" With programmable thermostats, setting the thermostat to regulate the temperature in your home based on the time of day is easier than ever, but does it really make that much difference?

Yes. If you have a standard furnace heating system, setting back your thermostat can result in energy savings. According to **www.Energy.gov**, "By turning your thermostat back 10–15° for 8 hours, you can save 5–15% a year on your heating bill." That means a 1% energy reduction for 1 degree lower setting. Not too bad. If you can set your thermostat back for an 8-hour period during the day while outside temperatures are warmer, you will probably not notice any difference in room comfort.

You May Not Want To Set Back Your Thermostat If...

There are several situations where you may not want to set back your thermostat. If you have an alternative heat source, a consistent temperature works better. Geothermal, baseboard heat, and radiant floor heating systems do not provide the same energy savings when the thermostat is set back on a regular basis. Most heat pump systems do not recommend using a programmable thermostat, because it can cause them to work inefficiently.

There are other factors to consider when deciding to set back your thermostat:

- age and condition of your home
- amount of insulation you have
- efficiency of your windows and doors

If there is a lot of heat loss while the thermostat is set back, it will take more time and more energy to get back to a comfortable temperature.

Know Your Thermostat

There are many different types of thermostats. Programmable ones are available in a wide range of prices and features (fig. 3.11). Some allow you to set a 5-day and 2-day block (weekdays and weekends) while some allow you to program each day individually. With some of the new wi-fi thermostats, you can make adjustments remotely from your smart phone.

FIGURE 3.11.
A programmable thermostat can take some of the work out of making your heating and cooling system run more efficiently.

Many people, especially during winter, ask, "Can you teach me how to use my programmable thermostat?" But too many just say "forget it" even if they understand it offers significant savings on their heating and cooling. Regardless of the type of thermostat you have, understanding how it works and its specific recommendations is very important. Please take the time to follow the instructions, so you get all the benefits from using it correctly.

Learning Thermostats

I don't usually talk about specific products because I like to remain neutral—and better products come out every day. But I installed a new product in my home, and I want to share my experience. It is the Nest Learning Thermostat, designed by a former Apple designer. It is elegant in design and simple to use (fig. 3.12a and b).

FIGURES 3.12A AND 3.12B. The Nest is a thermostat that learns from the temperature settings you choose.

This thermostat learns from the settings that you adjust to over time and remembers them. It really just does this for you. It can also be controlled from your smart phone, which is great because so many times I can't remember if I adjusted the temperature or I've been out-of-town for a few days and want to make sure it's not freezing cold when I get back. The Nest system may be more expensive than a traditional programmable thermostat, but I figure I'm going to pay for it in energy savings alone in just a few years.

Ceiling Fans

Install and use Energy Star rated ceiling fans. If you have it spinning 10 hours a day, you'll only use about 15 cents worth of electricity. The moving air from the fan makes you feel cooler, allowing you to set the thermostat a little higher (fig. 3.13). A fan can be a beautiful decorative accent as well. When it's not too hot outside, you can use just the fan, a freestanding fan, or a whole house fan instead of the air conditioner.

FIGURE 3.13. A ceiling fan can keep you cool for pennies a day. (And help keep you warmer in winter, too.)

For many people, ceiling fans are a must during the summer to keep cool. This is because airflow causes a wind chill effect that cools your skin. But most ceiling fans are left idle all winter, and you miss out on energy savings and a more comfortable home. The main reason people avoid using fans in the winter is the same wind chill effect. So which is it? Ceiling fans on or off in the winter? Some studies have shown that reversing your ceiling fan and using it in the winter can lower heating costs by 10–15%! That's a significant savings!

How Do Ceiling Fans Help Warm You in the Winter?

Everyone knows that warm air rises. Because of this, a lot of the warm air your heating system puts out goes to the ceiling, leaving the cooler air down on the floor level. Reversing your ceiling fan to pull the cool air up, forces the warm air to move out and down the walls of the room. This redistributes the heat and warms the entire room. Just make sure your ceiling fan is turning clockwise as you look up at it.

But what about the wind chill? Try the fan on the lowest speed setting. Just a gentle movement of the air can make a big difference. If you have high vaulted ceilings and your fan is on the low setting, it will push warm air down without you having to change the direction or feeling a chill down at the floor level. It just takes a little trial and error to find out what works best for you.

How Do You Reverse a Ceiling Fan?

In summer, the fan turns counter clockwise pushing air down. In winter it should turn clockwise. Changing the direction of most modern ceiling fans is easy. Turn off the fan to prevent the chance of being hit by the blades. Find the direction switch, usually located on the fan motor housing. Move the switch, (get off the ladder) and turn the fan back on.

Whole house fans

A whole house fan (called an attic fan in Oklahoma) pulls cooler air in through open windows and exhausts it through the roof. In combination with ceiling and freestanding fans, it might be enough to cool your house in hot weather. Whole house fans must be sized and installed by a professional. There is also a way to use the ducts of your HVAC system to provide whole house cooling, too.

Hot Water

There is nothing like a nice hot shower or bath to relax sore muscles or to warm you up. Having hot water in our homes via a spigot and not a kettle hanging in a fireplace has been one of the greatest advances in home technology in the last century. Because a water heater is one of the home systems we really rely on, it is important to know your options what it comes time to replace it.

The energy efficiency of your water heater can make a big impact on your household budget. According to **www.Energy.gov**, 12–20% of average home utility bills come from the water heater. There are several types of water heaters, but you have to start with the type of energy sources available to your home—gas, electric, and solar. Look for a system that has earned the Energy Star certification.

Storage Tank Water Heaters

The most common storage tank water heater is electric, with natural gas ones nearly as popular. These traditional water heaters store heated water in a tank and keep the water hot at all times, which means it is always on (fig. 3.14). Obviously, this is not a very energy-efficient method. Their popularity and volume also sets the cost of a new water heater fairly low.

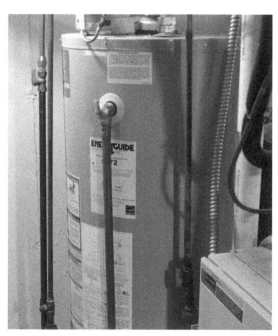

FIGURE 3.14. Storage tank water heaters are the most common type found in American homes.

Gas water heaters are typically more efficient than their electric counterparts. A gas water heater with the Energy Star qualification of high efficiency will use less energy than older models and can repay your investment with energy savings in three years or so.

Tankless (On Demand) Water Heaters

Tankless water heaters have been used in Europe for many years and are an up-and-coming alternative here in the United States. Instead of heating the water in the basement and piping it to the kitchen and baths, the heaters are placed on the walls in the kitchen and baths. They provide hot water immediately 'on demand' using natural gas or propane or electricity to heat water when the hot water tap is turned on. These very efficient water heaters never run out of hot water and are best suited for a household that uses 40 gallons of hot water or less per day. According to **www.Energy.gov**, they have been found to be 23–35% more efficient than standard water heaters. Even households that use more than 40 gallons of hot water a day still get 8–14% increased energy efficiency. There are Energy Star options.

Tankless systems generally cost more upfront. A gas line or a high voltage line will need to be run to the kitchen and baths to fuel the new units. Consult an HVAC professional when you are considering tankless units, because they are quite different from traditional storage systems.

Solar Water Heating Systems

The most environmentally friendly way of heating water in your home is with solar water heaters. Even with an upfront cost that can be double that of a tankless system, these innovative systems obviously cost much less in the long run because they use the sun's energy to heat the water—and that energy is free! There are federal tax credits on solar water heaters through 2021. Some states offer additional incentives through tax credits and local energy companies may offer discounts, too.

Heat Pump Water Heater

Heat pumps can do more than heat and cool your house, they can also heat water. Both air-source and geothermal heat pumps can perform these three functions. A stand-alone heat pump water heater has a water storage tank or can be adjusted to work with an existing water heater with a tank. Heat pumps work by removing heat from the air, so they are more efficient and effective in year round climates of 40°–90°F. Heat pump systems cost more, but they are efficient and have lower operating costs over the long run.

Saving Hot Water Saves You Money

Heating water is the second largest energy expense in your home, after heating and cooling. It accounts for about 18% of your utility bill. To conserve hot water, fix leaks, install low-flow showerheads and faucets, and purchase an energy-efficient dishwasher and clothes washer.

If your water heater has a storage tank, you'll see how heat radiates out and is lost while the water sits in the tank and also as it travels through the pipes to the kitchen and bathroom. It is pretty simple to insulate the tank and to wrap the pipes with insulating tape. This helps. If you're renovating or building new, consider adding a system that sends the cool water sitting in the pipes back to the water heater instead of letting it run down the drain while you're waiting for the water to get hot. Or you can keep a bucket or watering can in the shower and save some of the cool water to use elsewhere.

Consider these facts from **www.Energy.gov**: Washing dishes with the water running uses two gallons of hot water per minute. A fully loaded Energy Star dishwasher only uses 6 gallons per load. Can you beat that? Washing clothes uses 25 gallons of hot water per load. Okay, we can wash clothes in cold water and still get them clean, so that's an easy one. A 5-minute shower uses 10 gallons. You can buy low-flow showerheads and save 25–60% on hot water costs. You can replace the aerator (screw-on tip of the faucet) with low-flow ones. Some even have shut-off valves to stop the flow of water without affecting the temperature. Take the one you're replacing to the store with you to be sure the new one is the right size. Can you think of other ways to cut back on the amount of hot water you're using in the kitchen and the bath?

WaterSense Water Saving Resources

WaterSense, a partnership program with the U.S. Environmental Protection Agency (EPA), offers consumers tips on saving water and a directory of approved products and services, useful whether you are building a new home or replacing older fixtures. WaterSense products use a minimum of 20% less water than traditional toilets, faucets, showerheads, and landscape irrigation systems. In fact, according to their website, homes using WaterSense labeled irrigation systems can expect to save as much as 8,000 gallons of water per year.

Appliances

A great article[1] from The Shelton Group (**www.sheltongrp.com**) suggested that the United States is in for an appliance replacement boom caused by the stagnated housing market. Because so many people are staying in their current homes, there is renewed focus on home systems, which are likely to be wearing out soon. Appliance and home system manufacturers are well aware of the life expectancy of their products and are chomping at the bit for it to begin. The question is, are you ready? You can do your research online or in the store, but for every green home purchase, look for the Energy Star rating.

Planning For Home System and Appliance Replacement

If your home is less than 15 years old, there is a good chance that the appliances and home systems are as old as your home. Once these go beyond a certain age, there is no doubt they will begin to require repair or replacement. Being able to foresee these events will allow you to prepare (budget) for the inevitable costs that come with owning a home.

Replacement of items such as refrigerators, dishwashers, hot water heaters, and laundry equipment can be predicted as they near the end of their life cycles. It is a good idea to have them maintained—which will extend their lifespan—and evaluated periodically by a service technician. Make sure to ask if there are any regular wear issues that can be addressed now to prolong the life of the unit. Things such as the replacement of belts and motors are relatively easy fixes if caught early and can help prevent more extensive damage later on.

Home systems all share this one important quality: It is less expensive to maintain them than it is to replace them.

When you replace an appliance, buy an energy-efficient one wearing the Energy Star label.

Put a Budget In Place

The fact is that all home systems and appliances will have to be replaced at some point. Budgeting for the inevitable will reduce the shock and financial hardship that can come from needing to replace

---

[1] Jim Lyza, "The Great Replacement Boom is Coming!" *The Shelton Group* (blog), October 3, 2012, http://sheltongrp.com/the-great-replacement-boom-is-coming/.

a major home appliance or system. Maybe start an emergency home savings account. Take time every few years to obtain a price estimate on these items, so you know how much they are likely to cost and can adjust your budget accordingly. Knowing the current prices of things will help prevent unpleasant surprises when replacement time comes.

How Much Energy Does Your Stuff Use?

Ever wonder how much it costs for your spouse or the kids to hold the refrigerator door open while they're scrounging around for something to eat? Do you see dollar signs—and now, precious water, too—flowing out of your house?

There are tools to help you and your kids see that there really is a cost associated with standing in front of the refrigerator with the door open. With the assistance of the internet, you can find calculators to help you understand what the different pieces of our convenient lifestyle cost us. And they do all have a cost. We just keep bringing more cool electronic stuff into our homes and, even if they are more efficient, the cost for the energy to run each one quickly adds up.

Visit **www.Energy.gov** and use the Appliance Energy Calculator. It has drop down menus, so you can select the appliance. I checked the energy used by my cable box. A cable box usually uses 140 watts of electricity. The average cost of a kilowatt of electricity per hour is given, but I used the drop down box to select my state, which, unfortunately, has a higher cost than the average per kilowatt hour. Then I input the number of hours that my cable box is on (24) and the number of days (365) and the program computes the yearly cost for me. Some websites provide charts that compare the costs of several appliances, so you can get a feel for which ones use the most energy. Generally if the appliance makes heat, such as an oven or clothes dryer, it uses more energy than appliances that keep time or provide light.

Often, your local utility company will offer programs and/or calculators to help you estimate how much it costs you to power the appliances in your home.

You might visit **www.EnergyUseCalculator.com** to calculate electricity costs of individual gadgets and appliances. It tells you what it costs to run each appliance in your home. You might decide to turn the coffee pot off earlier tomorrow morning.

There is a way to get an accurate, on-the-spot reading, too: with an energy usage monitor, which you can buy at hardware stores for $25–50. You plug the appliance or gadget in question into this monitor, and it shows how much electricity the gadget uses. You cannot use these monitors on any appliance that uses 220 volts, such as clothes dryers or water heaters.

Reducing Phantom Electric Costs

Many appliances and electronics have a stand-by mode to allow a remote to be used or to keep settings or a clock going. They are using power even when they're on standby. This is called phantom load or vampire power. It's good to take this usage into account, too, as you're deciding when to keep them on and when to turn them off—or to replace them.

An easy way to reduce phantom power costs, especially with electronic equipment, is to use a power strip—or two! There are now power strips with multiple plugs divided into a section for devices that need to stay on and another section for devices you want to turn off after using them.

For instance, your wi-fi router is a device that you don't want to turn off, because it controls a lot of things in your home. You would plug the wi-fi router into the section that is always turned on. Your printer can be turned off without causing problems, so it is plugged into the section of the strip you turn off. Innovations like this make it easier to control and save electricity. If it's easy, then you are more likely to do it. That makes a lot of sense to me. Look for them next time you are visiting your favorite electronics store or website.

If you want to get the family on board, go to the energy calculator and show your household members how much money it takes to keep that refrigerator open for 5 minutes. It might change their minds if you take that amount out of their allowance every time they do it.

Home Energy Savings That Add Up

When it comes to home energy savings, electricity is the one that costs us the most. It is also the easiest for us to cut back on to save money. Electricity is a funny and interesting thing. You cannot see it, but it is still there. We pay thousands of dollars each year to have it in our homes and take for granted that it will be available when we need it. With all of the electronic devices we rely on these days, it is easy to overlook what it costs us to have these devices ready to go when we need them. Those costs add up quickly.

I recently ran across a cool info-graphic that shows that 75% of the energy an appliance uses happens when it's not being used. The graphic (at **www.homeenergysaver.ning.com**) compares the costs of wasted energy from common household appliances with each other and with the number of cases of beer you could buy with the money you're currently wasting on electricity. It does demonstrate how home energy waste—or savings—adds up.

Many people relate energy costs and electricity use directly to the lights in the house. This makes sense because light is the way we actually see energy in use. While turning off lights is one way to reduce energy use, there are quite a few other areas, as you have seen, that will save you a great deal more without you having to live in the dark (fig. 3.15).

FIGURE 3.15. Light is the way we actually see energy in use.

Don't get overwhelmed. Saving energy can be done one little change at a time. One useful website is **www.Energy.gov**, which provides a wealth of up-to-date information for saving energy, money, and time, such as tips for saving energy doing laundry and the best options in Energy Star washing machines when you need a new one.

Refrigerator Maintenance

"Hello, Is your refrigerator running?" "Yes." "Then you'd better go catch it!" That may be the oldest prank call in the book, but it's not funny when your refrigerator isn't running. Summer is the time of the year when I cannot wait to get home and get a nice, cold...anything really. It is hot and the fridge is the obvious place to go for a cold treat, but is your fridge running well?

If it isn't, try cleaning it. Refrigerators run by pumping Freon through condenser coils, similar to an AC. By cleaning the back of the fridge of dust and debris, you let the coils breathe and pull air more efficiently.

If your fridge is still not running correctly, you might look up videos or tutorials on how to diagnose the problem. Tutorials on Wikihow, like "How to Diagnose Refrigerator Problems" (**http://www.wikihow.com/ Diagnose-Refrigerator-Problems**), have tips including making sure the fridge is plugged in correctly, pulled far enough away from the wall, and that the vents are clean.

If you've cleaned and tried everything in the book and your fridge still won't work, it may be time to get a new one. Go online and look at reviews. Go to the store and try out models and see what you like and compare prices. Consumer Reports has a fridge-buying guide.

Buying New, What to Do?

What should you consider when buying a new home appliance? Beyond the look and design of home appliances, which is the first thing we think of, it's important to consider how efficient each product is with respect to energy and water usage. There are calculators online to help you compare new appliances. A great website to do research before heading to the store is **www.EnergyUseCalculator.com**. Always look for and buy appliances with the Energy Star rating!!

CHAPTER FOUR

What is IN Your Home: What to Think About, What to Look For, What to Choose

• • •

WE TURN NOW TO CONSIDERING what the things in your house are made of, such as wood, metal, glass, plastic, paint, varnish, and glue. How on Earth are you supposed to know which products are the best made, the most efficient, and the most Earth friendly? You can check online at various websites, especially of the nonprofits that set the standards for sustainable, eco-friendly products. (See *Resources*, page 133.) Of course, you don't want to bring VOCs or toxins into your home if you don't have to. But if you don't know they're there, then you might bring them home by mistake.

Don't worry, you don't *have* to do research before you can go to the store. Just look for the labels—Energy Star, WaterSense, GreenGuard and so on. These labels help you choose with confidence. Green labels show that a third-party has tested the product and issued a certification or rating to show that the equipment/product meets certain criteria in green and energy programs. The most common ones are listed in Table 4.1.

Flooring

As we think about ways we can make our homes healthier, for our families and for the environment, one thing we can change is what is under our feet. Flooring is easy to take for granted. We walk, roll, crawl, lay, and play on the floor every day, typically without a thought or care about it, until the time comes that you have the need to shop for it. There are hundreds of choices, and like most things in life, they all have pros and cons. You just need to focus on what is going to work

TABLE 4.1 Green Labels

Carpet and Rug Institute	Carpets and Rug Institute Green Label
Energy Star	Energy efficient appliances and home products
Forest Stewardship Council (FSC)	Forestry products (lumber, wood floors, paper, etc.)
Green Guard	Products that promote healthier indoor air quality
Green Seal	Products - environmental responsibility
Green-e®	Certified renewable energy programs
KCMA Environmental Stewardship Program	Cabinetry
National Fenestration Rating Council (NFRC)	Windows and glazing
Sustainable Forestry Initiative (SFI)	Forestry practices
WaterSense	Plumbing and water conservation

best for you based on personal preference, performance, fashion, and lifestyle. And you do even with paper products, you need to consider manufacturing methods and carbon footprint—how much energy it cost to make that flooring and to get it to your house.

Wood

I like to think of hardwood flooring as furniture for your floor. It is a classic look that can be used in most design styles. It is easy to clean and maintain, but it is not indestructible. There are factors that can make some woods better choices or better performers than others if the floor is in a high traffic area or you have pets in the house. The more grain, color variation, and character a floor has, the more it can hide surface scratches. I stress this point for households with pets. The less shiny a floor is the less light it reflects, so the less it shows dirt, wear, and imperfections. For people who like the look, texture also hides more imperfections. Texture can be created by hand-scraping, wire-brushing, or distressing. Basically, textured floors already look worn, so they wear—or hide their imperfections— very well. Choosing a color for any floor is personal preference, but in general, very dark floors will show more dust, smudges, and footprints. They may not be the most practical color for large families or busy people. I like to compare them to driving a black car: it looks great when it's clean, but it is going to look dusty or dirty sooner than medium to lighter tones.

Bamboo

Bamboo gets lumped in the category of hardwood flooring, but it is actually a grass. Since it can be re-harvested about every seven years, it does frequently get classified as a "green" product. However, I like to point out that by being a grass, bamboo has to go through a fairly hefty manufacturing process in order to become a floor. In addition, most bamboo flooring is made in China, so for customers here in North America there is a much larger carbon footprint associated with bamboo when compared to a regionally local solid hardwood.

Traditional horizontal or vertical grain bamboo is similar in hardness to southern red oak. It will perform similarly to a clear grade domestic maple wood, in that there is not a lot of graining or color variation and can show more surface scratches and imperfections.

Strand bamboo is a shredded bamboo that is re-pressed together with glues and resins, which makes it very hard and gives it more of a "graining" effect. I do consider strand bamboo to be a better choice for pets in the home when compared to horizontal or vertical grain, however it can still scratch and cannot be completely re-sanded and refinished like a solid hardwood because of the way it is constructed.

Cork

Cork flooring is a wood product, because cork is the bark of a tree. The bark can be re-harvested about every nine years and harvesting does not kill the tree, so cork is considered a good environmental choice. Although some think of it as a new fad, cork flooring has been around for a very long time. There are cathedrals and churches with cork floors that are over 100 years old. Cork is your softest hard surface and gives you the best thermal and acoustical value when compared to other hard surfaces. Cork can be scratched or gouged like a wood, but is harder to dent because its cell structure is flexible. It is also naturally insect repellant and mold and mildew resistant, which is why Dom Perignon started using the material as a bottle stopper in the 17th century!

Stone and Tile

Stone has been used for centuries as a flooring material. It is very durable—think of the 2,000 year old stone mosaic floors in Pompeii and Roman villas. It is also cold and smooth. These are desirable qualities if you live in the tropics where it is always warm outside, and you enjoy the coolness of stone underfoot, but marble and stone are so cold in the winter. (Radiant heat can make you love tile again.) As for carbon footprint—unless the quarry is next door, stone is heavy and costly to transport.

Tiles have also been used as flooring for centuries. My favorites underfoot are Saltillo tiles from Mexico. They are unglazed and feel good to bare feet and, over time, wear into smooth curves. These look homey and inviting, but tile has a cool elegant side, too. Easy to clean and to maintain—just don't drop the cast iron skillet. But if you do, it's relatively simple to remove the broken tile and to replace it, as long as you still have leftover tiles.

Stone and tile floors are good choices for homes where allergies or asthma are a problem. They don't emit gases or chemicals, and they are easy to keep clean. They're also good with pets. One of my friends had three Doberman pincers—large, active dogs. Her family room had a floor of natural bluestone tiles that are used outdoors for patios and walkways. She could hose it out if she needed to.

Tile comes in two types, ceramic and porcelain. Porcelain is more expensive for several reasons. It is harder and does not absorb water and the color of the tile goes all the way through, so chips are less noticeable. If you are going to put the tile in a high traffic area, such as kitchen and bath, porcelain is the most durable choice. Lay the tiles you are considering down on the floor and stand on them. That's how you'll see them in your home, not propped up on display shelves.

Other Flooring Options

There are an amazing variety of flooring choices ranging from stone to wood to carpet. To help organize your search, you want to look for green qualities in every kind of flooring: natural, low-emitting (of toxic chemicals), and local. Natural wool carpeting is greener and healthier than conventional carpet, which has a large carbon footprint and lots of toxic chemicals. If you prefer hard floors, consider cork, tile, bamboo, or natural linoleum. Those seeking hardwood floors might consider recycling the hardwood floors that other renovators are getting rid of. When buying new, make sure your hardwood is FSC-certified or Sustainable Forestry Initiative (SFI).

When replacing carpet, look for the Carpet and Rug Institutes, Green Label Plus certification of low-VOC carpet materials and adhesives. Additionally, when replacing the carpet, caulk (using a low-VOC caulk) along the floor where the wall meets the floor (fig. 4.1). This will reduce air leakage and help with energy efficiency.

FIGURE 4.1. Caulk along the crease where the wall meets the floor.

Reduce, Reuse, Recycle

Once you have a good floor under your feet, you can think about all the items you bring into your home—how they are made, what they are made of, and how you can extend their useful life, even after you are done with them. I hope you will find ways to recycle and reuse building materials and furnishings and decorative elements in your green home. It's a creative approach with an environmental payoff.

The Third R: Recycling

Recycling is the third R in the very green motto "Reduce, Reuse, and Recycle." We start with recycling because we already own these things, so what do we do with them when we no longer want them? Recycling is a gateway to greener living and often the first action that leads to others. In St. Louis county, where I live, single-stream curbside recycling is offered for the entire county. Years ago, when curbside recycling was first introduced, I'd fill up my bin every week and my trash got smaller and smaller. The neighbors started asking how I was getting so much into the recycling bin and so little into the actual trash. I had researched what could go in our recycling bins and was putting in everything I could. When neighbors asked, I would share with them what I'd learned, and before long, the other recycling bins started filling up, too.

Actually, recycling has been around for a long time. When I was a kid, I'd go up and down our street with a wagon collecting newspapers to raise money for some cause or group. Paper has been recycled for a long time and is relatively easy to recycle. Wood and its by-products, including wood pulp, are used a number of different ways as wood and paper products. Manufacturers are finding ways to use by-products of one process in another product. (Especially when we consumers are buying those products made of recycled material. Manufacturers need a good reason to do it.)

Paper Goods: Look for Products Made with Recycled Content

The easiest stuff to buy recycled is paper products, including paper towels and toilet paper. Though, it may be tough to convince others in your household to use toilet paper made from recycled content. But good options are out there. Look around at stores where you might not normally think to buy paper products. Even a store like Office Depot carries a quilted 100% recycled-content TP for little more than 25 cents per roll if you buy the jumbo 48-pack. Or shop online!

If you can't find a 100% recycled toilet paper that meets your needs, search for manufacturers that are being good environmental citizens. Look for the Forest Stewardship Council (FSC) logo for companies that responsibly source the wood they use. I read an article about Kimberly Clark working with Greenpeace (**http://www.greenbiz.com/ blog/2014/10/06/kimberly-clark-and-ngos-building-sustainable- supply-chain**) to address issues raised about their sustainability practices, mainly fiber sourcing. The two large consumer product companies, Kimberly Clark and Proctor & Gamble, both have quite a bit of sustainability information on their web sites. I applaud their efforts and hope they will continue to do even more, especially using more recycled content. As for me, I will continue to buy and encourage others to buy recycled content whenever possible. Keep in mind, the bigger the demand for recycled products from consumers, the more manufacturers will supply—and that is good for the planet, as well as all of us who live here.

Think Before You Throw Away

When you throw something away, where is away? In our minds, the trash is just gone. But in our world, away is a dump or a landfill site—or worse yet, the ocean—and we are running out of places to put our trash. If you haven't been to a landfill or dump, I recommend you go to see firsthand where away is. Away takes up land and uses energy, time, and more resources to deal with our discards. The more ways we find NOT to throw things away, the better. This is contrary to our lifestyle of convenience and our habit of throwing things away when we are done with them. Disposable is convenient since we don't have to deal with it, someone else does. It also appears that many products are designed to be thrown away rather than to be repaired—electronics, appliances, cars, etc. Slowly this situation is changing. For example, if you have an Apple product, the company will reclaim and recycle the plastics, metals, and glass in it. This is an environmentally friendly practice that needs to become common in every line of manufacturing.

"If it can't be reduced, reused, repaired, rebuilt, refurbished, refinished, resold, recycled, or composted then it should be restricted, redesigned, or removed from production."

—PETE SEEGER, folk singer and social activist

Reduce first (buy less), then reuse (over and over), and then recycle (last resort)

Just because a disposable item can be recycled, doesn't make it a better choice than a reusable item. Little steps add up! Because we do need to recycle, we need to make it easy to do. Single stream recycling makes it easy so people don't have to figure out what can or cannot be recycled. It all goes in together. Curbside recycling makes it even easier to do. Signs and labels help people to know what can go in the recycling stream. Typically, single stream recycling is a great fit for household everyday stuff—paper, cardboard, aluminum and tin cans, most plastics (check the number in the triangle on the bottom), and glass.

Then there is the hard to recycle stuff because it contains metals or toxic chemicals—printer cartridges, electronics, plastic bags (grocery bags, cleaner bags), CFL bulbs, batteries, and more. In many areas, schools or libraries collect some of these hard to recycle items for fundraisers. Many big box stores and electronic stores offer recycling for electronics, CFLs, and other hard to recycle items. Grocery stores collect plastic grocery bags and other film plastic bags. Hazardous products like paint and motor oil need to go to a collection center. Tires are usually recycled by the shop selling you the new tires. A great resource for hard-to-recycle stuff is **www.Earth911.com**. This website offers a search tool for recycling just about anything. There are lots of articles on recycling and green living, too.

If you can't recycle something, try to reuse or re-purpose it. At minimum, donate it. Get creative about keeping stuff out of the landfills. The quote I heard so often when I was growing up from my grandmother is actually a New England proverb, "Use it up, wear it out, make it do, or do without."

A mindset change is in process. We are changing from throwing everything away to a mindset of repair it and make it last. A mindset of bartering goods and services and making art out of things people used to throw away. Whenever possible, look to buy items that can be repaired or at least reused, repurposed, or recycled. Since buying and selling things is associated with making money, a mindset shift about money may also be needed. Mindset changes come over generations and over time. It's time.

Let's all take action to use our resources more efficiently. Recycling not only keeps things out of our landfills, it also saves material, energy to produce it, and water used in production. It almost always takes more (of everything) to produce a product from virgin materials. Starting with material that is even partially processed, saves steps and energy.

Buying recycled items encourages manufacturers to offer more recycled products and at better prices. Oftentimes, traditional products are being subsidized, so they cost less than their recycled counterparts. But we all pay a higher environmental price for using them.

Upcycling: A View of the Future

As William McDonough and Michael Braungart point out in their book Cradle to Cradle: Remaking the Way We Make Things, in nature there is no such thing as waste. Every output of one process in nature is an input for another. Upcycling is the new perspective they offered to the world in 2002, when the book was first published, and slowly but surely that concept is gaining ground in practice. By the way, their book is printed on a plastic polymer "paper" that can be upcycled into new books and other products. By comparison, a book made of paper doesn't have much of a future.

A non-profit organization, Cradle to Cradle Products Innovation Institute (**www.c2ccertified.org**), issues Cradle to Cradle certification by assessing the materials that make up an item in five categories: material health, material reuse, renewable energy, water stewardship, and social fairness. The goal is circular—materials that can be cycled forever. Wow.

Recycling is about much more than bottles and cans

There are many ways to recycle used goods. You can reclaim parts of old houses, like bricks, wood floors, mantels, doors, and doorknobs. You honor the work of craftsmen from earlier eras and the virgin forests that were cut down to build homes when America was young. If you are fortunate enough to live close to a business that salvages parts of old buildings, including windows and doors and iron railings from the porch, you have a gold mine. Other places I have found salvaged parts of houses are the Habitat for Humanity ReStore and Salvation Army, but the pickings are scarce. Many old houses are just torn down and no one carries off the riches that lie within. You can search online for Salvage and Property Services or companies that dismantle old barns and save the wood. Sometimes, there are houses being renovated in your city, and, if you ask, you might be able to have the wood flooring or some other element for your house. It is a satisfying (and inexpensive) way to find quality materials for your own home. I met with Steve Weise, a Washington builder of green homes, at his own home to see how he had used reclaimed materials, siding, and rafters from an apple bin canopy that he moved from Portland and reassembled in Cowiche, Washington. His is a zero-energy house.

Re-Loved Furniture

For years, I've tagged along with my mom while she explored a handful of furniture resale shops in Oklahoma City where she lives. I could not seem to find the same kind of stores in St. Louis. I don't know if I wasn't looking hard enough or a bunch of them popped up at the same time, yet now they seem to be abundant. Furniture resale shops are a treasure! Buying gently used furniture is not only easier on your wallet, it's a great way to keep furniture out of the landfill and honor the quality work of older generation craftsmen, not to mention finding one-of-a-kind pieces that can make your home pop!

I kept passing The Refind Room—one of the furniture resale stores in my town. I finally stopped in and what a treasure I found. The owners, Shawn and Suzanne, visited with me and told me more about their sustainability actions and how that works with the store. One seating ensemble in the store includes pieces from 14 homes and still looks like it was all meant to go together. One of the things I love about going to a store like this is the decorating and furnishing ideas you can get, especially from the people at the store.

There are many options for buying used furniture—vintage and second-hand stores, garage sales, estate sales, Goodwill and Salvation Army, and online. I like the idea of a store where I can see the furniture in a setting, making it a bit easier for me to envision how it could look in my own home. I also like having the "vetting" that a store may provide with their criteria for accepting furniture for sale or consignment.

I also perused the internet for some tips on buying used furniture. I used the search phrase "why buy used furniture" to find sites with some good advice. A few recommendations stand out.

- With upholstered furniture, check for odors, pet hair, and stains. Turn the chair over or tip the couch back and look underneath to check the frame for good quality construction.

- Imagine the piece as it might look with your personal touches or paint or varnish.

- Choose a low- or no-VOC paint or stain.

- Check online for any recalls to the children's furniture you're considering buying used.

Second-hand furniture can add a new dimension to your home, and hunting for the right piece can be an adventure on its own. Enjoy. And remember that you are helping yourself, the community, and the world.

CHAPTER FIVE

Landscaping

• • •

WHEN WE CONSIDER HOW to keep our homes cool in the summer, most of us think about how to change the indoor temperature. Air conditioning! But one of the best ways to keep your house cooler starts outside. Strategically placed trees and shrubs can enhance the beauty of your home—and save you money. Yes, the landscape around your house also has an effect on your energy and water bills. Take a walk around the house and consider these points:

- Where does energy flow into and out of your house? Where are the openings in the building envelope? Every window and door is an energy flow point, but so are the holes cut into the foundation to connect to the air conditioning unit or to bring in the TV cable.

- Could trees and shrubs help reduce unwanted energy flows into and out of the house? Awnings and trellises fall into this category, too, because they block sun, wind, and water.

- How and where do you use water outside? Do your water bills go way up in the summer? How could you cut back on water use?

Driveways, sidewalks, and patios can be energy savers in the winter if they are dark and absorb heat from the sun and release it slowly, warming the air around your home. In summer, that passive solar activity is not so good. If driveways are light colored and reflect sunlight, they will keep the area around your home cooler. If you are going to put in a walkway or a path around your house, consider making it with gravel or mulch, because rain and snow can soak through these materials and into the ground. Water sheets off paved surfaces and runs down the drain. You want to save precious rainwater for your trees and plants and lawn, so you don't have to use fresh drinking water to water them. Rain gardens and rain barrels are an attractive and effective way to save rainwater and use it when you need it.

Rain Gardens

Rain gardens are a beautiful way to keep water on your property (being useful) rather than letting it run off and become a flood or carry pollutants into streams and rivers. The more trees we cut down to build housing developments and the more land we cover with pavement, the more flooding we have. So, while it may be small, a rain garden makes a difference—and rain gardens all over your city will make a really big difference! A rain garden is planted in a shallow bed and fills up with a few inches of rain, allowing it to slowly filter into the ground and nourish its water-loving plants. Rain gardens filter 30% more water into the soil than a regular lawn does.

Your rain garden is important because it helps

- protect lakes and streams from lawn chemicals, oil, gas, and other pollutants.
- replace ground water and refill local aquifers.
- protect your community from floods.
- beautify your yard and the neighborhood (curb appeal! See fig. 5.1).
- provide habitat for birds, butterflies, and honeybees.

FIGURE 5.1. A rain garden is a beautiful way to keep water on your property.

Trees and Shrubs

Take a look at the trees and plants around your house. Do the bushes planted around the foundation protect the walls of the house from the wind, especially where there are openings? Oftentimes the foundation plants that the builder put in years ago have grown too large and are causing problems rubbing against and damaging the siding or the roots are growing into the basement. You'll need to dig them up and replace them with plants that will serve as windbreaks and shade but not grow too tall to be right next to your house.

You might plant one or two trees to provide shade to the sunniest side of the house and help keep your house naturally cool (fig. 5.2). Check out how tall the tree will be when it's full-grown and the shape it will have. Don't plant too close to the house, again with consideration for roots damaging the foundation or interfering with pipes going into the house.

FIGURE 5.2. Trees provide welcome shade and cooler temperatures on the sunny side of the house.

Now, with all this planting of bushes, be aware of the location of the air conditioning (or heat pump) unit. Don't plant large bushes right next to it; keep this area clear to help the unit operate efficiently. On the other hand, the AC unit benefits from being in the shade. Maybe an awning or trellis? Get professional advice before planting near it, because it makes a strong warm breeze when it's operating, and this might damage plants growing too near.

Water in Your Landscape

How does water use impact your bill? Do you have an automated sprinkler system? Is it set to water early in the morning or in the evening? These are better times to water your lawn because less water is lost to evaporation. There are WaterSense sprinkler systems that use 8,000 gallons less than a regular system. Better than sprinklers, though, are soaker hoses buried underground because the water is not sprayed into the air where it evaporates in the sun. The roots get watered well, and you use less water with soaker hose systems.

Where else do you use water outdoors? In the garden? Again, soaker hoses, rain barrels, and watering cans are the best way to go. My neighbor got a deal one summer on six huge plastic barrels. I watched as every barrel filled and overflowed in one of our big storms, which frustrated him, but he did succeed in keeping a lot of the rainwater on his property, and he had a full ration of water for the vegetable garden for the next month. His barrels sat on concrete, but you can put them on gravel, mulch, or pavers to keep from making a muddy mess.

Do you wash your car in the driveway? Some communities do not allow this because oil and gas and other chemicals get swept down the drain. If you can wash your car at home, do you use a hose with a shutoff spray nozzle, so the hose doesn't run the whole time you are soaping the car? Remember that's drinking water you're using.

As many people know all too well, heavy storms bring lots of water rushing down the gutters and downspouts. Does that water drain well away from your house or do you get a wet basement or "lakes" in low points in the yard? What do you do with all that water? You can extend the drainage from the downspout out into the yard with those black plastic hoses. You might need to dig near the foundation and place French drains under the ground to carry water away from the house. Those low point lakes are in your yard, because the soil is not absorbing water. You might dig out the clay and replace or mix it with sand and compost, so the water can soak in. This is not a place to put a rain garden until you do something about the drainage problem.

Lawn and Garden Maintenance

Consider how your garden grows—with sun and rain and wind and rich soil. So far, so good. A lot of advertisers want you to believe that the only way to have a beautiful lawn and garden is to use the chemicals they want to sell you. But there are eco-friendly—bird, bee, and human friendly—ways to make your lawn and garden grow without those chemicals. I encourage you to try them. All the chemicals you put on your lawn (millions of pounds of them in America every year) find their way into our water supply. These chemicals genetically alter or kill fish and aquatic creatures and plants that are part of the closed water system on this earth. This may be one of the most damaging activities of any homeowner—maintaining a green, weed-free lawn at all cost. The cost is steep, my friends.

Having a lawn might be one of the silliest things we homeowners do. We spend time, money, water, chemicals, and energy to encourage plants to grow so we can mow them down. Many homeowners are choosing to have more garden area, including edible gardens and native plants, and a much smaller lawn—with maybe a grass strip between garden beds. Think outside that big green box of lawn! (See figure 5.3.)

FIGURE 5.3. Let your lawn go. Gardens are prettier and easier than lawns to maintain.

If you have a lawn, consider what kind of grass it is. Kentucky bluegrass, for instance, is gorgeous—in Kentucky where enough rain falls to keep it green and growing. In Colorado, Kentucky bluegrass is more like a crime against nature. There is not nearly enough rainfall in the high desert of Colorado, so automatic sprinklers are always going strong. And meanwhile, the farmers and the cities out there are fighting over who gets to use the water. So, consider the rainfall patterns of your area before you choose the kind of lawn to have. It should be no surprise that Xeriscaping, or landscaping with plants that require no watering, started in Denver, Colorado.

I'm planning on using deep root Pearl's Premium grass, which is like buffalo grass, in my back yard. It only needs mowing once or twice a month and, once established, is drought resistant and requires no chemicals. There are other grasses that make similar claims: No-Mow

Lawn Seed, EcoLawn, and Pennington Smart Seed. Zoysia grass is touted as never needing mowing.

You can use organic fertilizers to help your lawn and plants and trees and garden grow. You could even start a compost heap if you have enough room—so vegetable peels and coffee grounds and grass clippings will be transformed into fertilizer. But you may not be interested in doing that much work. Don't worry, you can buy organic compost, too. There are green lawn care companies that use few or no chemicals. Where there's a will, there's a way. I hope you will find the way to be happy in your yard and happy with its impact on you and on the environment around you.

Native Plants for Green Landscaping

Continuing the focus on energy efficiency, you want to choose plants that work in harmony with nature, plants that

- thrive in your area of the country
- require little maintenance or water
- attract wildlife
- help control invasive species

Native plants are a great choice. They don't need chemicals, fertilizer, or water. They save you water, time, and money while providing a habitat for birds, butterflies, and other wildlife. Most of all, native plants don't need you to spend a lot of time working in the garden (fig. 5.4).

FIGURE 5.4. Native plants don't need chemicals, fertilizer, or water—or your time.

All gardens are green, but the "greener" ones make good use of native plantings. Here are some of the key benefits of creating a landscape with native plantings.

- *Low maintenance.* Native plants have survived in your area without help for a long time.

- *Little or no irrigation.* Native plants have adapted to the available moisture in your soil along with your local weather patterns.

- *Little or no herbicides.* Native plants have survived without poisons. They attract insects and microorganisms that keep the plant naturally healthy, so there is no need for herbicides.

- *Wildlife habitat creation.* Native plants create an environment that attracts a diverse array of birds and butterflies.

- *Beauty.* Native plants offer summer flowers and fall foliage. You can have a delightful and colorful landscape using a majority of native plants.

- *Long term savings.* Native plants are hardy, reducing the need to replace plants in your yard.

- *Reduce invasive species.* Native plants help prevent the invasion of non-native species that threaten endemic plants, grasses, and bushes with extinction.

You don't have to rip up your yard to start a native plant project—you can do one section at a time. You shouldn't have any trouble finding beautiful and hardy native plants at your local nursery, because more and more homeowners are thinking of ways to live more environmentally conscious lives.

GREEN LANDSCAPING TIPS

Here are a few tips to help you get started on your green landscape.

- **To find nurseries with native plants** search the internet using terms such as *native planting, natural landscaping,* or *green landscaping*. Remember to add your geographic location to the search, (e.g., native plants in New England.) Please don't go out and collect wild native plants—what if you took the last one?

- **Before you start buying**, check out the plants you already have. Which plants are native to your area? Which plants need no extra water? Now, which ones do you plan to replace? Have fun. Take a local nature class to learn more about plants native to your area. You might include the whole family in your search and gardening activities.

- **Planning is essential.** Plants have specific needs in terms of sun, shade, and water. You need to take into consideration the height and width and blooming times for flowering plants. Whether you prefer a manicured look or a more casual garden, try native plants. You can design landscaping that includes plants around the perimeter of your home, deck, or patio that will grow to just the right height. My favorites are the lilac bushes near the deck, where I can enjoy their fragrance as warm weather brings us outdoors again.

- **Remember that first year plants are never at their best,** so be patient. The second and third year will bring bounty and beauty to your landscape. Take photos each year, so you can see where additional plants are needed, and where current ones need to be cut back or moved or contained. Perennials should be separated every three to five years, but the good news is that you'll have new plants to put in other areas of your yard.

- **While you can get many garden design ideas from websites and books and magazines, it's a good idea to work with a landscaper** from your local area, too. Native plants vary widely from one part of the country to another. The landscaper will test your soil, give recommendations for natural plant choices, show you photos of lovely natural landscaping, and know where to find the right plants for you.

CHAPTER SIX

Maintain and Document so You Can Rely On Your Home

• • •

Homeowner Education and Documentation

As a homeowner, you've taken on a big responsibility. The good news is that there are many of us out here offering you a hand with learning what to do, keeping track of what you need to do, and documenting all that you have done. Maintenance tasks are part of every homeowner's life, whether you live in a castle or a cave. It is an investment of your time that pays back huge dividends and saves you lots of money down the road—and makes you money when it's time to sell your house. So, why do maintenance? It's the smart thing to do.

As you see in the *Maintenance Checklists* (page 94), documentation keeps you organized—and sane. When you keep track of what you need to do and write down what you have done, you can sleep well at night, knowing that the roof is not going to leak and the air conditioner will keep on blowing sweet cool air.

User Manuals: Who Needs 'Em?

You do. We all do. Maintenance and repairs are much easier if you have saved the user manuals that come with every system from HVAC to garage doors, and with every appliance and electronic gadget you buy. The average home in the U.S. has a minimum of 75 systems that are relied on every day, ranging from kitchen and household appliances to HVAC systems and lawn care equipment. Each one comes with a user manual. When the system or product comes into your house, write the purchase date and price and the serial number on the cover of the user manual. You will need this information someday. And then carefully place the manual into your household folder (or binder or drawer) with all the other manuals until you need them. And you will.

It might seem like a huge bother, but when something breaks, you'll wish you had the manual—even if it's just to find the model number to tell the repairman or to do an online search for trouble-shooting help. When you take a manual out to make repairs, write the date and the repair you did on the cover of the manual—or in the house notebook you're keeping. You'll need to know this next year—and the year after—and when you sell your house, the buyer will need to know, too.

If you are not handy and have never done any home maintenance—do not worry! How-to directions, videos, and tutorials are just waiting online. Here are a few of the home systems that require routine maintenance and/or periodic inspections.

Heating and Cooling (HVAC) System

Change the filter in your HVAC system quarterly (or monthly if dirt builds up) so it doesn't have to work so hard, which saves you money. This also keeps the air in your home cleaner, reducing the amount of dust that you breathe.

Make sure that your exterior air conditioner unit is clean and the area around it is clear of objects that restrict the flow of air. Because this system relies on airflow, it can quickly become choked with dust and leaves. Your local HVAC specialist can show you how to keep it free of debris.

Have a yearly inspection by a service technician. This simple, inexpensive step helps you avoid costly emergency repairs. HVAC specialists are trained to recognize potential issues and fix them before there is a breakdown. Ask the technician how often air is exchanged in your system, to be sure fresh air is being circulated regularly in your house. If you have a moisture buildup problem in your house, you may want to look into venting systems that monitor humidity in the room and open the vent to let in outside air when it is needed.

Exterior Home Systems

The exterior systems work to keep your home dry and comfortable. The roof, windows, siding, and gutters are the barrier between you and rain, wind, and extreme weather. Look for damage or changes you need to repair right now. Because of exposure to the elements, these systems deteriorate over time. It's easy to perform a visual inspection each month by taking a few minutes to walk around the outside of your home. Look for damage to siding and brick, raised shingles, sagging gutters, or anything that looks out of the ordinary. Contact a professional if you feel there is a problem.

Gutters and downspouts can fill up with leaves and debris, and then rainwater hits the dam and spills down the walls or backs up into your attic. It is essential to make sure gutters and downspouts are cleaned out each spring and fall. If it's too yucky, you might pay someone to do it, or you might invest in covers for the gutters that let rain through but not those leaves.

Garage Door Home Systems

Push the button, the door goes up, right? Well yes, but there are moving parts that can wear out. Check the manufacturer's instructions for areas that need to be lubricated and cleaned. Garage door openers also require periodic maintenance to keep them running smoothly.

Do Winter Maintenance While It Is Still Warm!

This may seem a little absurd, but, by the time winter arrives, you will be focused on the holidays and may have missed the opportunity to prepare your home for winter. In an effort to make sure that you stay warm and comfortable this winter, here are five home maintenance items to put on your to-do list before the holidays.

Windows and Doors

Inspect the seals around your windows and doors. Replace any worn or torn weather stripping. This is an inexpensive step that can pay big returns when it comes to heating your home. The areas around doors and windows can let cold air rush in and dollars flow out in the form of energy costs. And in the summer, the faulty seals allow your pricey air-conditioned air to escape.

Fireplace and Chimney

Having your fireplace and chimney inspected and cleaned, if needed, is much easier before it gets cold. Most people wait until they want to

TIPS TO UPGRADE AND MAINTAIN
YOUR GREEN HOME

Listed below are ten ideas to upgrade and maintain your home. The items listed start small and simple and end with larger scale projects.

$ = $0–$100
$$ = $100–$500
$$$ = $500 and up

1. **Keep vents clean and free of clutter or obstructions to help optimize efficiency.** This applies to HVAC air supply and return vents, dryer vents inside and outside of the home, and the vent under the refrigerator. ($/FREE)

2. **Install a programmable thermostat and USE IT!** The programmable features of the thermostat will only save money if it's programmed. Don't forget to set it to vacation mode when away from home for an extended period of time. ($)

3. **Replace incandescent bulbs with LED bulbs.** When upgrading lighting, look for Energy Star light fixtures. This is also a good time to seal air leaks above the fixtures by caulking or installing UL-rated covers to seal the light boxes. A wide variety of LEDs are available. It's ok to keep any CFLs you already have, but be sure to recycle them when replaced, and replace them with LEDs. Replacing bulbs with LEDs is such a quick payback, too. ($–$$)

4. **When updating bathroom or kitchen fixtures, look for low-flow options or WaterSense.** Shower heads that are 5 years or older can use 5–10 gallons or more a minute, whereas newer fixtures are available that use less than 2.5 gallons per minute (gpm). A typical ten-minute shower with an older fixture uses 50–100 gallons of water, whereas the low-flow fixture would use only 25 gallons. This could pay for itself in less than a year. Also look for low-flow aerators for the faucets or upgrade to new faucets, many with great warranties. ($–$$)

5. **When freshening-up a room with a new paint color, use low or no-VOC paints.** Almost all paint manufacturers offer full lines of low or no-VOC paints. ($–$$)

6. **Install ceiling fans.** The fan moves the air and makes occupants feel cooler, allowing you to set the thermostat a little higher. Installing a fan is a beautiful decorative accent as well. ($$)

7. **Install a sun tube to brighten up a dark area without using electricity.** Bathrooms, closets, and dark hallways are great places to install a sun tube. They're easily installed and bring the natural beauty of sunlight to a dark area. ($$$)

8. **Window treatments can look good and perform well by helping to control light and heat—protecting your furnishings and helping reduce your utility bills.** When updating window treatments, look for insulated options. Also, keep curtains or blinds open during the day in the winter to get the benefit of the sun and then close them at night to insulate against cool air. In the summer, close curtains during the day to prevent heat and solar gain. Blinds and curtains that diffuse or direct the light are especially helpful on east and west windows to help control glare. ($–$$$)

9. **When replacing carpet, look for the Carpet and Rug Institutes, Green Label Plus certification, which ensures low-VOC carpet materials and adhesives.** Additionally, when replacing the carpet, caulk (using a low-VOC caulk) along the floor where the wall meets the floor. This will reduce air leakage and help with energy efficiency. ($$$)

10. **When updating a kitchen or replacing appliances, look for the Energy Star and WaterSense labels.** Using appliances that are designed to be more efficient results in big savings over the lifetime of the appliance. Don't forget many areas offer old refrigerator haul-offs and recycling, too. ($$$)

use their fireplaces to have them checked, so chimney sweeps book up fast when the temps start to fall. Fireplaces can make a home feel cozy and homey, but they can also be dangerous if they are not inspected and cleaned regularly. A fire high up in the chimney can spread to your roof. Make sure to contact a certified chimney sweep as they are trained to recognize and correct potential fire dangers.

Roof Inspection

Inspect your roof. Note any shingles that look out of place or areas that appear damaged. Get a roofing expert to make a formal inspection to ensure that you don't have any issues when the weather turns cold.

Garage Doors

The seals around your garage doors can be damaged from the extreme heat of summer. Openers may need to be adjusted. Never attempt to adjust the high-tension spring. This is dangerous and should only be done by a trained professional.

Make Storage Space

A lot of items that are kept outdoors during warm weather need to be stored over the winter. Patio furniture, garden hoses and tools, and even plants can take up valuable space. Save yourself the pain of working with frozen fingers. Building storage areas and clearing out clutter is much easier when it is still warm out.

Seasonal Home Maintenance Checklists

*This section was written by Tina Gleisner, founder of The Association of Women Home Owners (**www.HomeTips4Women.com**).*

We've organized home maintenance into four seasonal checklists. At the beginning of the heating/cooling season, it's important to inspect and improve your home's envelope, so the money you spend heating or cooling isn't wasted. After heavy storms, inspecting your home and making timely repairs will avoid higher repair bills down the road if hidden moisture is eating away at your home's infrastructure.

- **Fall Home Maintenance** focuses on buttoning up your home for the winter and keeping you dry, warm, and comfortable.

- **Winter Home Maintenance** goes indoors to find and repair the minor, annoying things we try to ignore the rest of the year.
- **Spring Home Maintenance** gets you outdoors to find and repair storm damage and to prepare your yard for the growing season.
- **Summer Home Maintenance** looks at outdoor safety, living spaces, and landscaping projects from fences to bird feeders.

Home Maintenance Priorities

In every chore for every season, these are your priorities:

- The safety of those in your home.
- Water damage inside and outside your home.
- Energy efficiency to save money and reduce impact on the environment.

Tips for Using the Checklists

Most of us don't do our own car repairs, and we don't expect homeowners to do all the home maintenance either. Pick the items on the list that you want to do yourself and for those that you don't like or lack the skills, tools, or time, find reliable home professionals you can call on.

If you don't have any experience with home maintenance, find an experienced homeowner or home professional to "inspect" your home with you one or two times, until you get comfortable with what to look for. (I'm sure there are YouTube videos on this, too.) Doing an inspection is important, because how else are you going to identify what needs to be done?

Maintaining a home is actually a three-part ongoing process—inspect, maintain, and update. To help you keep track of what you've done and plan to do, make notes on the checklists.

- **Inspect.** If you've only got an hour to spare, pick one exterior side of the house or one room inside to inspect. Note the date you did this on the checklist and flag items needing maintenance or repairs, so you can schedule time or make a list for your handyman.

- **Maintain.** Keep your home safe (smoke detector batteries), energy efficient (furnace air filters), and prolong the useful life of many home features (caulking bathroom tile). Write it down when you complete a task. Keeps you from guessing later on.

- **Update.** Take advantage of improved materials and fixtures, upgrade to new building codes, and evaluate when it makes more sense to make an improvement rather than repair, such as replacing a bathroom floor rather than repairing the grout.

Fall Home Maintenance Checklist

Fall brings changes. School starts, and in much of the country, leaves turn color and fall to the ground; days get shorter and cooler. It's time for home maintenance. In the same way a coat keeps you warm and dry, your home's envelope (roof, siding, windows) protects you from the elements, keeping you warm and dry.

Keep Your Family Safe

With inclement weather, there are more chances for injury around the home. Make sure all entrance doors are well lit, handrails secure, and walkways and steps are in good repair. Indoors, it is a good idea to have seating where people put on and remove boots.

FALL HOME MAINTENANCE—HOMEOWNER TASKS		NOTES / DATES
EVERY QUARTER (or more often)		
Test smoke and carbon monoxide batteries monthly.		
Change furnace filters. If they're really dirty, change them more often.		
Clean humidifiers (especially important in the winter) and change filters per manufacturer's instructions.		
Clean dryer lint trap with each use. Once a quarter, clean vents and behind the dryer to remove lint buildup.		
EXTERIOR LIGHTS		
INSPECT	Check outdoor lights while ground is dry; replace as needed.	
MAINTAIN	Change any exterior lights that require use of a ladder.	
UPDATE	Switch to motion sensor lights or solar lighting to save power and provide security.	

FALL HOME MAINTENANCE—HOMEOWNER TASKS		NOTES / DATES
EXTERIOR WALKWAYS		
INSPECT	Walk outdoor paths looking for anything that might cause someone to fall, especially when the path is wet or covered in snow.	
MAINTAIN	Repair bumpy walks and cracks that might freeze and get larger.	
UPDATE	Consider snowmelt mats and driveway cables to melt snow and reduce slipping. Use eco-friendly alternatives to salt because rock salt erodes concrete and kills grass and goes down the drain.	
HANDRAILS INSIDE AND OUTSIDE YOUR HOME		
INSPECT	Test handrails to make sure they're secure.	
MAINTAIN	Add brackets where there are wall studs.	
UPDATE	Add extra handrails to assist anyone having difficulty with stairs.	
GUTTERS AND DOWNSPOUTS		
INSPECT	When it rains, check for leaks at gutter seams. When cleaning, make sure gutters and downspouts are firmly attached.	
MAINTAIN	Clean gutters after leaves have fallen and repair as needed.	
UPDATE	Add gutters or rain diverters over entry doors to minimize icy walkways/stairs underneath.	
SMOKE AND CO DETECTORS		
INSPECT	Test batteries monthly and replace immediately if you get a chirping sound.	
MAINTAIN	Replace batteries in smoke detectors once a year; replace detectors every 7–10 years. *Hint: A good way to remember to change your batteries is to do it every year when the clocks change.*	
UPDATE	Install carbon monoxide detectors to sense odorless, colorless gas coming from improperly burning fireplace, stove, water heater.	

Protect Your Home from Water Damage

Every year we experience weather events from extreme heat to high winds, heavy rains, and flooding, it's so important to make sure your home is safe from water leaks. Why? Wherever moisture levels approach 20% and there is a source of food, like wood, you are likely to find mold growing or carpenter ants. Worse yet, most of this damage can go on for years before it becomes visible. Repairs can be costly when you don't prevent or repair leaks quickly.

FALL HOME MAINTENANCE—HOMEOWNER TASKS		NOTES / DATES
ROOFING, VENT PIPES, CHIMNEY, AND MORE		
INSPECT	Inspect the roof while cleaning gutters (binoculars/camera can be used from the ground) or check the attic or upstairs ceilings for water stains. When a roof is 10 years old, get a visual inspection every year.	
MAINTAIN	Don't wait. If anything looks suspicious, make necessary repairs—missing shingles, cracked vent stack, or chimney flashing, etc.	
UPDATE	Get to know your roof and plan (budget) for replacing it.	
SKYLIGHTS		
INSPECT	Inspect ceiling and trim around skylights for staining. When on the roof, inspect the outside flashing for signs of wear.	
MAINTAIN	Condensation may occur with skylights, so a dehumidifier might be needed to reduce indoor humidity.	
UPDATE	Consider replacing skylights (average life approximately 18–20 yrs) when you get a new roof.	
SIDING AND MORE		
INSPECT	Visually inspect (binoculars if unable to get on a ladder) your home's exterior for signs of deteriorating paint or water damage. From the top down, inspect for signs of water leaks or damaged wood: • **Fascia**—vertical boards immediately under the roof. • **Soffits**—horizontal boards behind the fascia with vents into attic. • **Wood trim**—corner boards and other decorative pieces. • **Siding**—boards covering the outside walls of your house	
MAINTAIN	Caulk seams where different materials meet, for example, corner boards and siding. Paint before water can penetrate the wood.	
UPDATE	If you're not painting often enough or have to replace damaged wood, consider switching to a composite material that doesn't rot. Homes that require frequent painting are good candidates for vinyl or fiber cement siding.	

WINDOWS AND DOORS

INSPECT	Check flashing on windows and doors at the top, and at the bottom, check window sills and door thresholds.	
MAINTAIN	Caulk around windows and doors to stop water from getting in, and replace worn weather stripping. Painting is key to protecting wood trim around windows and doors.	
UPDATE	If you have persistent water problems, consider redoing the flashing, which might not have been installed correctly. For new trim, consider a composite material that does not rot and does not need painting.	

EXTERIOR FAUCETS

INSPECT	Make sure there are no leaks, which waste water and might freeze.	
MAINTAIN	Shutoff outside faucets. Remove hoses (critical for drainage) and cover with insulating jackets.	
UPDATE	Replace faucets with frost-free spigots.	

DECKS, PORCHES, AND STAIRS

INSPECT	Check the structural components (mostly hidden) of exterior wooden home features to ensure there's no wood rot. Probe with a screwdriver. The biggest problem area is where these attach to the house, because the flashing is often done wrong or is missing.	
MAINTAIN	Make sure flat surfaces have a way for water to drain off quickly. Clean weep holes or add them if there aren't any.	
UPDATE	For problem surfaces, or when updating a deck or other exterior structure, consider composites that do not rot.	

FOUNDATION

INSPECT	Walk around your foundation and make sure there aren't any places for water to pool and seep into your basement.	
MAINTAIN	Use splash blocks to direct downspout water away from your house. Maintain landscaping to ensure ground water runs downhill from the house, keeping a close eye on settling around new homes and excavation projects.	
UPDATE	Serious basement water problems may require extra drainage solutions from a sump pump to exterior foundation drainage with French drains.	

Save Energy, Money, and the Environment

Heating and cooling is the big ticket item of energy users. Tackle small projects each year, focusing on rooms where you spend the most time. Before updating your home, check for state and federal incentives and tax breaks. (Search online for Federal Tax Credits for Consumer Energy Efficiency and for State Tax Credits for Consumer Energy Efficiency.)

FALL HOME MAINTENANCE—HOMEOWNER TASKS		NOTES / DATES
PROGRAMMABLE THERMOSTAT(S)		
INSPECT	Check heating/cooling system turns on when you change setting.	
MAINTAIN	Review programming. Try lowering target temperature 1–2 degrees during winter (and 1–2 degrees higher in summer).	
UPDATE	Add additional heating/cooling zones.	
HEATING SYSTEM		
INSPECT	Stockpile filters so you can replace them monthly.	
MAINTAIN	Schedule your annual heating system.	
UPDATE	Discuss your furnace/boiler operating efficiency with the HVAC professional and get advice on when to replace parts or all of it.	
INSULATION AND VENTILATION		
INSPECT	Use a special thermometer to find where you're losing conditioned (warm or cool) air. Check for leaks from • your home's conditioned space to the attic or basement. • inside your home to the outside through walls and around windows, outlets, and wall switch plates. • ductwork and/or hot water pipes around your home.	
MAINTAIN	Replace insulation that gets wet and make sure vents are not blocked by insulation, as this will reduce effectiveness.	
UPDATE	Add more insulation to attic or exterior walls.	
WINDOW ENERGY EFFICIENCY		
INSPECT	Check windows and storm windows/doors for a tight seal.	
MAINTAIN	Swap screens for storm door panels; install storm windows or similar barrier to slow air transfer.	
UPDATE	Add more energy efficient windows (double and triple pane) or have your handyman build custom plexiglass storm windows, which are helpful for a sunroom as it gives you a longer season and slows heat loss.	

WINTERIZE AIR CONDITIONERS

INSPECT	Air conditioners (window and central AC systems) and clean.	
MAINTAIN	Remove window air conditioners and store for winter. Cover outside condenser units with a special cover made to fit the unit, or secure by wrapping heavy plastic sheeting around the unit.	
UPDATE	Monitor improvements in energy efficiency. Compare product costs to annual operating costs. Replace when the new unit costs can be recovered in a few years.	

Winter Home Maintenance Checklist

Keep Your Family Safe

Winter offers an opportunity to sit down with your family and go over home emergency situations. For example: what should they do if a water pipe or valve fails and the kitchen is flooded? Show everyone where shutoff valves are located and how to use them. Know how to shut off water to appliances, toilets, and showers. Know how to shut off the power to any part of the house. Practice what to do and have a plan. Prevention and preparation take time, but they give you peace of mind and prevent accidents.

WINTER HOME MAINTENANCE—HOMEOWNER TASKS	NOTES / DATES

EVERY QUARTER (or more often)

Test smoke and carbon monoxide batteries monthly.	
Change furnace filters. If they're really dirty, change them more often.	
Clean humidifiers (especially important in the winter) and change filters per manufacturer's instructions.	
Clean dryer lint trap with each use. Once a quarter, clean vents and behind the dryer to remove lint buildup.	

WATER HEATER

INSPECT	Test the temperature and pressure safety relief valve according to manufacturer's instructions, at least once a year.	
MAINTAIN	Drain your hot water heater once a year to remove sediment from bottom. Have the anode rod replaced every 3–5 years.	
UPDATE	Set hot water temperature to 120° F to protect from scalding.	

STAIRS AND TRIPPING HAZARDS

INSPECT	Check stairs and railings and look for tripping hazards around the house and garage.	
MAINTAIN	Tighten screws and secure anything that is loose. Organize sports, gardening, and outdoor equipment for easy and safe access. Hang ladders horizontally so children do not climb on them.	
UPDATE	Build shelving, install hooks, or install a storage solution to keep things organized. Add lighting wherever there are changes in elevation.	

ELECTRICAL

INSPECT	Review electrical outlets/fixtures to ensure they're working properly. Wiring that sparks when turning lights or appliances on/off should be repaired immediately by a licensed electrician.	
MAINTAIN	Repair electrical outlets or fixtures that aren't working. Add outlet covers if there are small children in the house.	
UPDATE	Upgrade old electrical system. Upgrade to ground-fault circuit interrupter (GFCI) outlets near water in baths and kitchens.	

CHIMNEY (for your fireplace and furnace/boiler)

INSPECT	Inspect chimney and vents annually and clean as needed.	
MAINTAIN	Have creosote buildup removed from the chimney by a certified chimney sweep. Close fireplace dampers tightly when fireplace is not in use.	
UPDATE	At some point you may need to install a chimney liner.	

INDOOR AIR QUALITY

INSPECT	Check that humidifiers and dehumidifiers are operating correctly. Search for any flammable or poisonous materials that pose a safety risk.	
MAINTAIN	Clean humidifier/dehumidifier filters weekly when using. Store dangerous materials in a high cabinet or behind a locked door.	
UPDATE	Dehumidifiers can be placed on a wall shelf to allow gravity-fed drainage into a utility sink to relieve you of having to empty the collection tank.	

Protect Your Home from Water Damage

Water plays a vital role in our lives but let's keep it where it belongs. The worst thing about water leaks is that they're hard to find!

WINTER HOME MAINTENANCE—HOMEOWNER TASKS		NOTES / DATES
SUMP PUMP		
INSPECT	Test the pump at the beginning of the rainy season and monthly thereafter.	
MAINTAIN	Clean out the pump annually.	
UPDATE	If you use the pump frequently, consider investing in a backup sump pump before you need it or a generator to keep it powered, so you don't get stuck with a flooded basement.	
BASEMENT		
INSPECT	Check basement walls and floors for dampness, leaks, mold, or white powdery deposits.	
MAINTAIN	Determine where leaks are coming from and repair as needed. Direct water from downspouts further away from foundation with inexpensive plastic tube extensions.	
UPDATE	Don't ignore leaking water in your home. Water damage and wood will invite mold or rot, and carpenter ants or termites.	
FAUCETS AND WATER HOSES		
INSPECT	Check for leaky faucets and make sure water/waste hoses to dishwasher, disposal, and washing machine are tight and not leaking anywhere.	
MAINTAIN	Replace worn/brittle washers in faucets or older hoses. Consider replacing entire faucet because once the first gasket fails, others will follow.	
UPDATE	Add shut-off valve at the hoses to your washing machine to turn off the water after use. Replace rubber hoses with flexible steel hoses.	
CAULK AND GROUT		
INSPECT	Check caulk and grout to ensure they remain water tight, and probe with a screwdriver to check for water damage.	
MAINTAIN	Replace caulk or grout. Check for underlying damage where there is any indication of a water barrier no longer working and repair the damage.	
UPDATE	Where you have frequent water problems, consider replacing with materials that aren't vulnerable to water damage, such as putting tile floors in an entryway or bathroom.	

Save Energy, Money, and the Environment

Home energy savings always start with heating and cooling. You can focus on small projects, and the results will add up.

WINTER HOME MAINTENANCE—HOMEOWNER TASKS		NOTES / DATES
HEATING SYSTEM		
INSPECT	Heating and cooling systems should be inspected and tuned-up by a HVAC professional once a year.	
MAINTAIN	Heating systems work best when filters are changed frequently; vacuum baseboards and air vents monthly.	
UPDATE	Review the cost/benefit trade-off of upgrading your system, because it can reduce fuel costs significantly. Adding additional zones to existing system can also help.	
ATTIC		
INSPECT	Check attic and attic stairs for heat loss.	
MAINTAIN	Insulate as needed, while maintaining proper ventilation in the attic.	
UPDATE	Replace worn out insulating materials.	
HEAT LOSS		
INSPECT	Have a home energy audit done, or do one yourself.	
MAINTAIN	Add insulation, ventilation, or home sealing. Recommend working with an experienced contractor.	
UPDATE	Replacing siding/windows provides greater comfort and energy use in the home and provides a good return on investment when you sell your home.	
REFRIGERATOR		
INSPECT	Check door to make sure it is airtight.	
MAINTAIN	Adjust latch as needed and vacuum coils twice a year.	
UPDATE	Keep refrigerator stocked, because a full refrigerator uses less energy than an empty one.	

Spring Maintenance Checklist

Spring is here. Time to get outside and enjoy the longer, warmer days. It's the perfect time to tackle some house chores.

Keep Your Family Safe

Always turn the power off before working on systems like your air conditioner. Check all your power tools and make sure they're working properly, with safety attachments in place. Unplug power tools when not in use and don't leave ladders up where children might climb them for fun.

SPRING HOME MAINTENANCE—HOMEOWNER TASKS		NOTES / DATES
EVERY QUARTER (or more often)		
Test smoke and carbon monoxide batteries monthly.		
Change furnace filters. If they're really dirty, change them more often.		
Clean humidifiers (especially important in the winter) and change filters per manufacturer's instructions.		
Clean dryer lint trap with each use. Once a quarter, clean vents and behind the dryer to remove lint buildup.		
YARD CLEANUP		
INSPECT	Check your yard for fallen objects, which could cause someone to trip. Check lawn mower blades and sharpen or replace as needed.	
MAINTAIN	Rake, prune, mulch, prepare garden for planting. Remove branches that are too close to the house. Service lawn mower before you need it.	
UPDATE	Improve landscape design features by adding walls, gravel walks, bushes, trees, gardens, etc.	
WALKWAYS, STAIRS, PORCHES, AND DECKS		
INSPECT	Check outside walkways, stairs (steps and railings), porches, and decks. Make sure everything is secure.	
MAINTAIN	Tighten loose boards and replace any that are warped or rotted and are a safety hazard.	
UPDATE	If more than minor repairs are needed, consider replacing stairs or deck with composite materials that don't rot and need less maintenance.	

SPRING HOME MAINTENANCE—HOMEOWNER TASKS		NOTES / DATES
AIR CONDITIONING AND HEATING SYSTEMS		
INSPECT	Vacuum baseboard heaters and schedule yearly check-ups for furnace and other systems.	
MAINTAIN	Service portable space heaters before putting away for the season. Empty fuel, clean, and store in a safe place.	
UPDATE	Upgrade to a more efficient heating system; add furnace humidifier if you don't have one already.	
EXTERIOR LIGHTING AND DOORBELLS		
INSPECT	Check exterior lights and doorbells, garage doors, and gates to make sure they are in good, working order.	
MAINTAIN	Repair any problems found.	
UPDATE	If there were any problem spots over the winter, add more lighting.	

Protect Your Home from Water Damage

Winter weather can be harsh on roofs, siding, and caulking, so inspect your home for any sign of leaks or damage that may have occurred. Fixing problems quickly can help you avoid a home's #1 enemy: water damage. You can also prepare for "April showers" by making sure your gutters drain away from your home's foundation.

SPRING HOME MAINTENANCE—HOMEOWNER TASKS		NOTES / DATES
ROOF AND ATTIC		
INSPECT	Check for loose shingles outside and for leaks inside the attic or top floor.	
MAINTAIN	Replace damaged or missing shingles. Clean and/or repair roof vents and replace damaged (wet) insulation.	
UPDATE	Replace roof. If you have ice dams, determine why and review options for preventing them next winter. Properly ventilated and insulated attics should not have ice dams.	
CHIMNEY AND VENT PIPES		
INSPECT	Check chimney, vent pipes, chimney cap, and flashing.	
MAINTAIN	Replace worn materials that have (or will soon) fail, such as when caulking gets dried out and cracks.	
UPDATE	Add chimney cap to reduce water getting inside and causing damage.	

SPRING HOME MAINTENANCE—HOMEOWNER TASKS		NOTES / DATES
GUTTERS		
INSPECT	Check gutters and downspouts to make sure they're draining properly and away from the house.	
MAINTAIN	Clean gutters and adjust/repair loose parts when you're cleaning them.	
UPDATE	Add covers to your gutters to reduce how often you need to clean them.	
SIDING, TRIM, AND EXTERIOR PAINTING		
INSPECT	Inspect wood (trim, windows, door kick plates) for peeling paint and gaps where water can seep in. Look for sawdust that indicates carpenter ants or termites.	
MAINTAIN	Paint wood trim more often than the entire house. Caulk gaps between siding and trim. Repair or replace water-damaged wood. Paint the side of your house with the most exposure to the elements (sun, wind, water).	
UPDATE	Re-paint the entire house when it needs it, not a year or 2 later, or you'll have more wood damage to repair. Upgrade trim to composite or non-wood product.	
WINDOWS AND DOORS		
INSPECT	Check doors and windows to make sure glass is intact and they're operating correctly and are weather tight.	
MAINTAIN	Re-caulk and replace weather stripping as needed. Replace broken glass and screens that are missing or torn. Swap out storm windows/doors for screens.	
UPDATE	Update windows and doors with more energy efficient ones to save on utility bills.	
DECKS		
INSPECT	Check decks, stair rails, steps, and other outdoor wood for rotted wood, nail pops, warping, or splintering.	
MAINTAIN	Repair damaged wood as needed. Clean, stain and/or seal decks annually.	
UPDATE	When extensive repairs needed, consider replacing with a composite material.	

SPRING HOME MAINTENANCE—HOMEOWNER TASKS		NOTES / DATES
WATER VALVES AND IRRIGATION		
INSPECT	Inspect hose bibs, pipes, shut-off valves, etc. Turn on outside water valves and irrigation systems carefully in case they froze and burst over the winter.	
MAINTAIN	Fix leaks and replace gaskets that are old and likely to crack soon.	
UPDATE	Make sure all outside plumbing can be shut off inside in case of a leak. Know how to respond to a burst pipe buried in your wall.	

Save Energy, Money, and the Environment

It's time to prepare for hot weather. Look at all aspects of your home that affect how comfortable you are indoors—screen doors and windows, air conditioners, and ceiling fan (hint: Counter Clockwise Cooler).

SPRING HOME MAINTENANCE—HOMEOWNER TASKS		NOTES / DATES
SCREEN DOORS AND WINDOWS		
INSPECT	Inspect storm doors and windows for any needed repairs before putting them away.	
MAINTAIN	Swap out storm windows and doors for screens, fixing any torn screens. Clean and store storm windows and doors.	
UPDATE	Replace missing window screens for ventilation. Consider adding storm doors for added sunlight and energy saving in winter.	
AIR CONDITIONERS AND HUMIDIFIERS/DEHUMIDIFIERS		
INSPECT	Install window A/C units or remove covers. Once installed, check to see that they're operating properly with no air leaks around the seal.	
MAINTAIN	Schedule annual maintenance for central air conditioning systems. Clean humidifiers/dehumidifiers and A/C filters.	
UPDATE	Add ceiling fans, wall A/C units, and/or central air conditioning to ensure your home is comfortable.	
CEILING FANS		
INSPECT	Are ceiling fans running smoothly and quietly so you want to use them?	
MAINTAIN	Change direction of your fan. You want the fan to turn counter clockwise to pull warm air up and away from you.	
UPDATE	Add ceiling fans to rooms where you spend lots of time to cut down on AC costs.	

SPRING HOME MAINTENANCE—HOMEOWNER TASKS		NOTES / DATES
HOT WATER HEATER		
INSPECT	Set temperature to 120°F or lower to conserve energy. Check temperature pressure relief valve. Ask heating (HVAC) pro to check critical components when tuning up your heating system.	
MAINTAIN	Drain once a year to remove sediment from the bottom of the tank or as recommended by manufacturer.	
UPDATE	Upgrade to a more energy efficient water heater and get the right size (# gallons) for your family.	

Spring Cleaning and Curb Appeal

There are always some miscellaneous items that don't make the other lists to deal with, and some that just make sense to tackle when it's warm outside.

SPRING HOME MAINTENANCE—HOMEOWNER TASKS		NOTES / DATES
POWER WASH		
INSPECT	Do your vinyl siding, decks, and porches look clean? Inspect for mold (green or black) that needs to be removed. Do not power wash shingles on the roof.	
MAINTAIN	You can pressure wash vinyl siding but not wood, because it will streak where the paint isn't adhering well, and you'll have to repaint or stain the wood.	
UPDATE	Replace exterior wood trim to reduce ongoing maintenance work (scraping and painting) with plastic or composite elements or wrap with aluminum.	
CLEAN OUTDOOR FURNITURE AND MORE		
INSPECT	Determine what needs to be cleaned up for spring/summer.	
MAINTAIN	Clean windows and put up awnings. Clean yard furniture. Pick up debris around downspouts and vents, remove tree limbs, and wash garbage cans.	
UPDATE	Purchase storage for organizing outdoor clutter, such as sports equipment, gardening, and more.	

Summer Home Maintenance Checklist

Summer is for fun. If you take care of home maintenance in June, you can enjoy the rest of the season. You want to protect your home from damage by ensuring that the exterior envelope remains water- and airtight.

Keep Your Family Safe

Summer safety focuses on cleaning up after storms, landscaping, and outdoor barbeques. It's also ideal for routine maintenance on your well and septic system.

SUMMER HOME MAINTENANCE—HOMEOWNER TASKS		NOTES / DATES
EVERY QUARTER (or more often)		
Test smoke and carbon monoxide batteries monthly.		
Change furnace filters. If they're really dirty, change them more often.		
Clean humidifiers (especially important in the winter) and change filters per manufacturer's instructions.		
Clean dryer lint trap with each use. Once a quarter, clean vents and behind the dryer to remove lint buildup.		
PREVENT STORM DAMAGE		
INSPECT	Identify tree limbs (unhealthy, leaning on or over house) that might come down during storms. After each storm, make a quick inspection to identify any downed branches and/or damage.	
MAINTAIN	Cut down dangerous trees/limbs before they cause damage. Use a professional tree service if the tree or branch might fall on your home when it's cut down.	
UPDATE	Before you plant: Check tree's full-grown height and address how the roots could affect your foundation and water pipes or septic system.	
DRIVEWAY, PATIO, AND WALKWAYS		
INSPECT	Check hard surface areas for cracks or holes.	
MAINTAIN	Repair holes and cracks larger than a hairline.	
UPDATE	Extend the life of your asphalt driveway with coating every 3–5 years to protect from damaging sun (should be done in warm weather).	

SUMMER HOME MAINTENANCE—HOMEOWNER TASKS	NOTES / DATES

LAWN MOWERS, OUTDOOR GRILLS, AND MORE

INSPECT	Check that mower blades are sharp. Inspect grills before first use.	
MAINTAIN	Get lawn mower serviced (oil, lubricate moving parts, replace spark plugs, fuel filters, air filters). Clean and fix outdoor cooking equipment.	
UPDATE	Upgrade to a higher efficiency, more environmentally friendly mower.	

WELL WATER

INSPECT	Check water pressure, signs of hard water, calcium buildup, etc.	
MAINTAIN	Test well water every year (EPA recommendation), because many contaminants have no taste, odor, or color. Use a state-certified laboratory.	
UPDATE	See if well-water problems can be solved with water filtration system.	

SEPTIC SYSTEM

INSPECT	Look for signs of trouble: odors near the leach field, sewage or wet areas surfacing, house drains flowing slowly, gurgling noises, or plumbing backups.	
MAINTAIN	Keep trees from growing on or near leach fields. Don't allow cars to park on leach fields, and never pave over them. Get your tank pumped out every 3–5 years, depending on house size and number of people living there.	
UPDATE	Ask your septic service provider to assess your tank and leach fields on each visit to plan for any major repairs before they're needed.	

Protect Your Home from Water Damage

Summer is a great time to look for problems stemming from excess water, moisture, and the pests that are attracted to moist environments. Address these problems quickly!

SUMMER HOME MAINTENANCE—HOMEOWNER TASKS	NOTES / DATES

TERMITES, CARPENTER ANTS, CARPENTER BEES, WOODPECKERS, SQUIRRELS, ETC.

INSPECT	Look for evidence of carpenter ants, carpenter bees, or termites: damaged wood, little piles of sawdust, termite shelter tubes (used to travel between wet spots). Woodpeckers go after pests they hear in your wood trim, and squirrels make homes in attics.	

TERMITES, CARPENTER ANTS, CARPENTER BEES, WOODPECKERS, SQUIRRELS, ETC. (continued)

MAINTAIN	Call an exterminator or animal control. Repair damaged wood and caulk cracks/gaps that let water and pests in. Eliminate any wood that touches dirt.	
UPDATE	Replace wood with composite materials to reduce pest problems.	

FOUNDATION PLANTS AND MULCH

INSPECT	Review foundation plants for adequate ventilation—not too close. Good air circulation ensures that water evaporates. Check mulch to make sure water is running away from your foundation (6-inch slope for the first 10 feet).	
MAINTAIN	Prune shrubs that are too close to the house and move mulch that may cause problems.	
UPDATE	Use shredded rubber mulch or crushed rock if termites are common in your area. These cost more but last longer, saving you time and trouble in the future.	

STANDING WATER

INSPECT	Walk around your foundation and yard after an average rain. Identify standing water that needs help to drain. Make sure water from downspouts drains well away from the house	
MAINTAIN	Downspouts may need to have French drains buried underground to move water at least 10 feet from your foundation.	
UPDATE	If you have excess water, consider planting trees, shrubs, or plants that use and thrive with excess water.	

MOLD, MILDEW, AND MUSTY ODORS

INSPECT	Check moist areas inside your home to see if you have a mold problem.	
MAINTAIN	Mold requires professional cleaning and the removal of the source of moisture (vent bathrooms and dryer outside, address moisture in crawl spaces, concrete slabs, etc.).	
UPDATE	Use a dehumidifier to remove excess moisture. Invest in a humidity tester (available at hardware stores).	

SATELLITE DISHES AND ANTENNA

INSPECT	Check satellite dishes and antenna to make sure they're attached securely and the connections are watertight.	
MAINTAIN	Secure and caulk to make sure no water gets into your home from these openings.	
UPDATE	Consider more creative solutions to mounting these fixtures.	

Save Energy, Money, and the Environment

You want to get the most out of your air conditioning.

SUMMER HOME MAINTENANCE—HOMEOWNER TASKS		NOTES / DATES
CENTRAL AIR CONDITIONER		
INSPECT	Check for shrubs and debris that could reduce airflow around the air conditioner.	
MAINTAIN	Change disposable filters or clean the washable filters once a month. Keep AC units clear of weeds, overgrown landscaping, and debris (turn the power off first). If you didn't have the units serviced in the spring, schedule that now.	
UPDATE	Monitor utility bills when using air conditioning and research the costs and benefits of new energy-efficient units.	
DOORS AND WINDOWS		
INSPECT	Check doors and windows to make sure they're airtight when closed. Is the caulking old, cracked, or missing?	
MAINTAIN	Replace weather stripping and/or caulking where you find air leaks.	
UPDATE	Consider double-pane windows to improve the comfort of your home during hot weather—start with windows in the two rooms you use the most.	
WINDOW COVERINGS		
INSPECT	Walk through the house in the morning and see where the sunlight is coming in. Check window treatments.	
MAINTAIN	Add shades, curtains, or window tinting to windows.	
UPDATE	Consider upgrading to automated window coverings.	
AWNINGS AND SHADE FROM TREES		
INSPECT	Identify rooms getting too much sunlight.	
MAINTAIN	Make sure awnings and/or trellises are stable and trim shade trees that are too close to the house.	
UPDATE	Review options for reducing sunlight in terms of cost, benefits year round, and aesthetics. For example, awnings work well in the back of a house but rarely in the front.	

Keeping Records Saves You Grief and Bother

Your life is simpler when you keep records on your house and what you do to it. There are many ways to keep records, from a three-ring binder to an online file, whatever works best for you. If you'd like to try it, my website **www.HomeNav.com** can help you keep track of the maintenance checklists and other paperwork associated with your home systems. You can store, organize, and access the information when you need it. The best part is that you also get instant connection to the manufacturer, industry experts, and their advice on each of your specific home systems.

Home Documentation Helps in Selling Your Home

When you buy a home, there is little information on the history of the building itself. Sellers typically provide only the information they are required to. There is no format to demonstrate maintenance or to document upgrades, repairs, or service providers. Any information provided is usually from memory or comes in stacks of receipts and user manuals after the home is purchased.

In short, the new homeowners are purchasing blindly. If you are selling your home, the more information you can provide, the more you can ease buyers' fears and make your home more attractive. The information you keep in your three-ring binder or that you have collected online enables you to provide potential buyers with detailed information on the home's maintenance and history. This gives the buyers the details they need in one organized place.

Once the home is sold, you can transfer the HomeNav account information to the new homeowner. The new owners can then access the file to find what services have been performed and which service provider performed them, which makes managing their new home easier.

There is a lot that goes into buying and selling a home. Providing potential buyers with a complete owner's manual adds to the value of your home and reduces the unknowns and fears that influence home buying decisions.

Home Disaster Recovery Plan

Several years ago as Hurricane Sandy was unleashing her power, I was participating in a Sustainable Disaster Recovery Conference, hosted by the St. Louis University Center for Sustainability, where we learned of resources available to people dealing with disasters. The devastation from the hurricane left thousands of homeowners and residents scrambling to find basic necessities and wondering where to turn for assistance. It took some of them a year or more to rebuild their homes. Some homes have never been rebuilt.

While none of us ever want to face a home disaster, they do happen. When they do, our first priority is safety. The second is recovery. Creating your home disaster recovery plan before you need it can help get things back on track sooner. This is not a disaster preparedness plan with emergency kits and go bags to help you survive. A home disaster recovery plan focuses on rebuilding and reconstructing your home.

You will be faced with many questions. Rebuilding your home from memory can be difficult, and replacing the contents may be next to impossible without a virtual backup of your home. Having a recovery plan provides a roadmap to identify, repair, or replace the lost or damaged contents of your home and the structure itself.

What Should Be In A Home Disaster Recovery Plan?

These are some of the important items that can be left behind or destroyed in a home disaster. These items are invaluable for both immediate and long-term recovery.

There are online tools and apps designed to help you store and organize all of this information in a secure, web-based account. Look for one that is flexible, so you can store whatever is important to you. The Federal Emergency Management Agency (FEMA, **www.fema.gov**) offers advice and suggests actions you can take now to ensure your family is protected should you be faced with a home disaster. Their smart phone app is useful, too.

- Homeowner's insurance policy and agent contact information
- Emergency and family contacts

- Home inventory
- Financial information: bank account information, investment documents
- Copies of credit cards and bank cards
- Trusted contractors and utility providers
- Copies of important personal identification documents: driver license, passports, birth certificates, marriage license, social security cards
- Pictures and videos of the contents and components of your home
- Home floor plan
- Receipts and user manuals for home contents

Other items you might want to include

- Family photos and videos
- Contact information for preferred service providers
- Links to other data that is important to your family

While no one can be completely prepared for the unknown, your home disaster recovery plan provides the peace of mind of knowing where to begin on the path to recovery.

CHAPTER SEVEN

Building
(or Renovating to Achieve)
a Certified Green Home

• • •

Your Dream Green Home

Dreams fuel my goals, personal and professional, and help me to think of what's possible. One of my big dreams is to build or renovate my own Dream Green Home. I recently did a Dream Green Home workshop, and it was so cool to see people's reactions. Many of them said they had never thought about their home in this way or about turning their dreams into goals. So, what elements would be in yours? Where would it be? How big would it be? How would it make you feel to live there? They had such fun exploring all the possibilities. Treat yourself to some dreaming. If you look at the money, time, and effort we spend on our homes, it is obvious they mean a lot to us.

For some people, a dream green home would be off the grid with no electric bill and no mortgage, and water from a well and cisterns, but still have every modern luxury. That is doable, but you sure need a plan. Other people want a traditional style home with every efficient system built in. Dream big, dream small, but dream. You might start with the Zero Energy Ready Home builders' challenge houses at **www.Energy.gov** to see super energy-efficient homes in every part of the country that will surprise and inspire you.

You can work with a builder, even a builder that builds hundreds of homes, as long as you have a roadmap and understand what you want. If you haven't set your own priorities, when you talk with a builder, you could end up jumping into all of the decisions, selections, and choices without understanding how they accomplish your goals and dreams. If this happens, your dreams may never get to be a part of the plan. You end up just taking what is offered, rather than leading with your priorities. I know a couple that looked for two years before finding the right area and a builder, who was already building a small group of houses. Using his floor plan, they moved the basement steps from the narrow hallway to the bedrooms into the garage and widened them, so there was plenty of maneuvering room to get all of their tools and equipment into the basement. The builder was so delighted, he made that change to all of his floor plans.

The Green Home Certification Process

A certified green home is independently verified to meet the requirements of a green home program. While many homes have some elements of a green home, only a small percentage have gone through the process to be certified as a green home. This situation is changing. As the number of home buyers looking to capitalize on the benefits of owning a green home continues to rise, homebuilders are putting more emphasis on eco-friendly construction and design.

You need to make the decision to build (or renovate to achieve) a certified green home right from the start. It will affect design, construction, and materials, and all will need to be documented. Each certification program has their own set of guidelines, but all lead to green certification. Choose one that you think will work best for your home. Follow these are the steps to get your home certified:

1. Choose a certification program.
2. Select a green homebuilder and/or consultant.
3. Set project goal and do an initial scoring run through.
4. Register project with certifying organization.
5. Conduct a rough inspection during construction.
6. Assemble supporting documentation of the home for the verification process.
7. Perform testing.
8. Final verification and submittal of documentation to the green certification program.

What Are Certified Green Homes?

To be certified, green homes must meet a defined set of practices and principles that are set by the industry. There are two nationally recognized green home certification programs in the U.S. They are the National Green Building Standard (NGBS) Certification Program from Home Innovation Research Labs and the Leadership in Energy and Environmental Design (LEED) program developed by the U.S. Green Building Council (USGBC). Both provide stringent standards and practices to follow for certifying a green home building (or renovation) project and offer resources to help complete the certification process.

There are also local, regional, and specialty green home certification programs. To find additional information about green home certification programs, check out organizations like Green Seal (**www.greenseal.org**) or search for green certification programs in your area.

The Benefits of a Green Certified Home

The concrete benefits that remain at the core of the green home philosophy are health and safety, comfort, cost savings, and re-sale value.

Healthy and Safety

For many of us, one of the most important benefits of a green certified home is that it is healthier and safer for the people who live in it. Improved indoor air quality is provided through exhaust and fresh air ventilation, the V in your HVAC system. Kitchen, bath, and clothes dryer exhausts are a must. Fewer pollutants and contaminants also contributes to improved air quality.

Comfort

A comfortable home means more than the recliner in the family room. We enjoy a home that is warm or cool when and where it should be, free of drafts, and with a humidity level that is appropriate for the climate we live in. Achieving this balance is a cinch in a green certified home.

Cost Savings

A green certified home ensures the envelope of the home (walls, roof, windows, doors, and floor) is well sealed and insulated to help keep the "conditioned" air we pay for inside the home. A well-insulated home with the right-sized efficient HVAC system becomes a comfortable, healthy, safe, super cost-saving package. Energy efficient hot water, lighting, and appliances contribute even more to the total savings. (Many of the homes in the Zero Energy Ready Home builders' challenge at **www.Energy.gov** have utility bills ranging from $30 to $6 a month.) Other factors also contribute to the cost savings of a green certified home. Durable materials and components contribute to lower maintenance and less need for replacements.

Re-sale value of your Green Certified Home

Green certified homes often have excellent resale value. From a *Washington Post* August 26, 2011, article[2], "In a study covering existing and new houses sold between May of last year and April 30 of this year, the Earth Advantage Institute, a nonprofit group based in Portland, Ore., found that newly constructed homes with third-party certifications for sustainability and energy efficiency sold for 8% more on average than non-certified homes in the six-county Portland metropolitan area. Existing houses with certifications sold for 30% more." Please note that the home must be certified by a third party. Certification offers proof that buyers will get what they pay for. While location, the economy, and property values are always key in real estate, a green home may sell faster and for more.

With the rapid growth of Green MLS (multi listing services) and Green Appraisal services in cities across the country, documenting and sharing the green and energy-efficient features of your home helps you to get top dollar when you are ready to sell your home. Green is here. Are you ready?

Building an Affordable Green Home

Many elements of green homes have already become common practice, because they just make sense. I would have to say that the biggest advantage to any green home building project is that it gives

---

[2] Harney, Kenneth R., "Is green good for home resale value?" *Washington Post*, August 26, 2011, https://www.washingtonpost.com/realestate/is-green-good-for-home-resale-value/2011/08/19/glQAMUGzfJ_story.html.

everyone involved an opportunity to see and evaluate the latest technologies and practices. This leads to the discovery of smarter construction methods for more efficient and affordable homes and reduces the impact a new home has, and continues to have for many years, on the environment.

Three areas provide the focus for an affordable green home project: sustainable planning, green design and building techniques, and owner/tenant education and documentation. Even if your everyday green home is not a new build or a complete renovation, these will still apply. Here are some examples of elements that might be included in each area.

Sustainable Planning

The planning process is the single most important element of an affordable green home project (or any project, for that matter). Thorough research in the planning stage gives you and your builder valuable information that makes implementing green elements much easier. You might go to the library and look through their collection of books on houses of all kinds. You might travel through the internet and be surprised by new ideas that architects and builders and homeowners have come up with. The more research you do, the quicker you can make decisions for your own home. This comes in handy when something goes wrong (not that anything ever goes wrong), and you have to shift to a new product or a new layout or a new something and you have to make a decision right now.

A few years ago, I worked with an architect for a 3-home affordable green project. This was his first certified green project. He commented on how astonishing it was that the project was able to meet the requirements of the National Green Building Standard (our chosen program) without being complex or a big hurdle. He and I agreed that the upfront work that went into the plans and specifications helped to attract a builder that could really do the job well and establish a great working relationship. Matter of fact, the three companies went on to do another project together.

The planning process has three goals:

- Design with the end in mind. (We designed and built to meet the Bronze level of the National Green Building Standard under the Green Building path.)
- Incorporate sustainable or green and energy efficient design, building, and materials.
- Reduce operating, utility, and maintenance costs.

Green Design and Building Techniques

Green design has to begin with the lot and site where your home will sit and how it will interact with the land around it. The natural landscape can play a big role in energy efficiency. Use the compass and the landscape to dictate where to place the house. The orientation of your home will affect where you decide to put windows and what kind of windows (and window coverings) to use. The project team usually helps figure out how the house and land will interact and the best site for your home.

Resource Efficiency

St. Louis, the Gateway to the West, was exposed to a wide variety of cultural influences, and this is displayed in the architecture. But, those pioneers had to build with the resources available locally (stone, timber, clay) and not waste anything—which is called resource management. This is why homes in New Mexico are built of adobe and homes in New England are built of stone and timber. These materials are readily available and are durable in the climate of the region. Resource management to save money and be eco-friendly is why we plan so carefully before starting to build. When the builder works with the client, plans for green building and resource management are usually correctly implemented.

You can save time and money and lessen your impact on the environment by choosing local materials and building a right sized house. Our project was under 1500 square feet. We used roof trusses that were trucked in and quickly raised. In fact, we chose several building components that required no additional site finishes: windows, siding, gutters, porch railings, and columns. This saved money and time on the build and is more resource efficient.

Ample porches provide shade and protection from the weather and from water getting into the house. (Hooray, porches are back!) The roof was designed with deep overhangs to provide shade to the interior and to protect the walls from water. We also used a water resistant exterior barrier, "house wrap."

If you're going to build where there is already an existing house, deconstruct it, and donate all the usable home components. In many communities, Habitat for Humanity sells donations in their ReStore to raise money for the homes they build.

Energy Efficiency

Once you have chosen a design, you want to be sure that the building envelope is well sealed and insulated. With a new build, putting in insulation, such as blowing in foam, is easy, but with a renovation, it is more difficult to get insulation where you need it. It is worth the extra work to be sure your house is insulated well.

Starting with the walls or the "skin" of your house, it is important to control air-movement throughout your home. Air will always go from hot to cold areas and from wet to dry. So, the barrier that makes up the outside of your house must be able to keep hot air out when it's cold inside, and moist air out when it's dry inside. Your builder or remodeler needs to understand this concept to maximize your home's insulation efficiency. For instance, check to make sure the builder caulks and seals the seams and joints of your walls and home. This air-sealing allows you to take full advantage of your insulation. Otherwise, it's like wearing a down coat with the zipper open.

There is a growing trend among builders to spray-foam the joints and seams near the foundation of the house, which is beneficial to the general insulation of the house as a whole. Some people insulate under the floor of the basement, or even wrap the foundation. It is also important for the builder or renovator to seal all the seams of ducts that carry heated and cooled air. At the top of your home, the attic is a critical source of heat transfer and must be properly insulated and air-sealed.

Of course, you have chosen an energy efficient HVAC system, but take time to consider some of the more technical questions, such as where will the vents in each room be? How much air exchange can there be in a large room with only one vent for intake and one for exhaust? Do you want vents high or low on the wall or in the floor? New systems have high-powered blowers and can use very small vents, and even hide them in the soffit of the room. Will the exhaust fans in the bathroom actually carry the moisture outside? These are the kinds of decisions that will be important to your comfort and your health. Having the right professional in your camp will help you get the system you want. Be willing to ask the hard questions, it will pay off.

You might also look into a geothermal heat pump for heating and cooling if the size of your lot, the subsoil, and the landscape will allow it. Geothermal heat pumps take advantage of consistent ground or water temperatures, so they can reduce energy use by 30–60% and control humidity. They are sturdy and reliable, and fit in a wide variety of homes. Geothermal heat pumps, unlike air-source heat pumps, can be used in extreme climates, and customers are happy with their performance. Also, new high-efficiency heat pumps use excess heat from the cooling mode to heat water. They can heat water 2 to 3 times more efficiently than an electric water heater.

You can heat your home using radiant floor heating or wood (or pellet) stoves. Look at the options. I've heard it said that a super-sealed house could actually be heated with a hairdryer. If you use a system like radiant floor heating, you'll need to ventilate the house naturally and add a humidifier or dehumidifier to get the right moisture balance inside your home. Get an energy professional to work with you so you get the right system for your home.

Of course, in your new green home, all the appliances, lighting fixtures, and ceiling fans will have Energy Star certification.

Water Efficiency

All the plumbing fixtures and toilets are WaterSense certified or provide low-flow/low-water usage. And outdoors, you do not have an irrigation system because your landscaping does not need watering.

In many developments, we still see clear-cutting of the trees to install the infrastructure—sewer, water, storm water runoff, and utilities. While other options are available, this is still the most common way. If you can convince your contractor to save all or some of the trees, you will benefit and so will the land around you. (I know a woman who stood in front of the heavy machinery on her property and insisted that the trees be saved. She won. The trees won. The air we breathe won. The land won. The watershed won.)

How to manage storm water is a big consideration in many communities, including St. Louis where our aging infrastructure is a factor. Better management of watershed areas (creeks and rivers) is helping, but you can help, too, by doing what you can to keep storm water on your property, so it soaks into the ground rather than running off, which adds to flooding. Flooding is a growing problem for communities all across the country. Trees and gardens help hold the water, but so do gravel driveways and mulch paths instead of paved ones. At the very least, consider a rain garden for your yard and use a rain barrel, or two! If you want to go a step or two further, consider a rainwater cistern. It could be underground or an above-ground tank. In areas where water is scarce or when disaster hits, this can be a life-saving and garden-saving addition to your green home.

Lawns first became an element of home ownership in the 18th century when British gardeners (landscape artists) developed them as part of the sweeping landscape around the great houses of the royals and landed gentry. (Did you watch Downton Abbey?) In the 21st century, you probably don't have a staff of gardeners, but you don't have to have a lawn, either. We sure do spend a lot of time and money growing plants that we just mow down. Instead you could have flower and vegetable gardens with paths of grass or pea gravel or mulch in between. You won't need fertilizer, seed, or weed killer. You won't even need a lawn mower.

If you are looking to do something innovative—look up! You might install a green roof of plants on part—or all—of the roof. Too much? How about a white roof to reflect heat? Using light colored roof shingles helps reflect heat. In fact, using light colored concrete or any paving material around the house helps reduce the heat of summer. Use a common sense approach with the choices you make for your home.

Indoor Air Quality

You will control how many and what kind of pollutants are used in the building of your house, especially VOCs through choices of low-VOC paints, adhesives, and flooring choices. The design will include exhausts in kitchen and baths to move pollutants and moisture out of the home, and the dryer will be vented to the outside. The houses we built did not have garages, which reduces exposure to harmful exhaust.

It is important to have team members that understand building codes (even if you are remodeling on your own, follow the building codes to avoid problems when you want to sell). Certain parts of the project, like electrical and plumbing, are the places to get professional help. A green professional adds to the project team and can ensure that green, sustainable, and energy-efficient components are integrated smoothly into your project.

Owner/Tenant Education and Documentation

Your green home will work only as well as you operate and maintain it. Proper operation is essential. The builder may put together a binder for you, but if he doesn't, be sure to collect and keep in a safe place all the information and resources you will need to take full advantage of the investment you have made in your home. As I've said before, you can keep it all in a three-ring binder or in a file online. Go online and explore your options.

Choosing your community

For most of us, our home sits on a street in a neighborhood. Ideally there are sidewalks throughout the community and people walk and bike, and children play outside (figs. 7.1a and 7.1b). Some communities go farther in encouraging community participation in activities at a town center and in community gardens. As people become more environmentally and holistically aware, there is a movement to reduce the time spent commuting and to work closer to home. For those who grew up in urban areas this isn't new, but the concept of having everything you need within walking distance is becoming much more appealing. While that means less fuel, less pollution, less water use, less wear and tear on our automobiles, the biggest benefit of using shoes rather than gas and tires is that we are healthier!

FIGURES 7.1A AND 7.1B. Location, location! Our homes are more appealing and we are healthier when nature and outdoor activities are within easy reach.

Paying for your Dream Green Home

Now that you know what you want, you need to figure out how to pay for it. There are many resources to help pay for new homes and remodels. You have to invest some time to find the resources and fill out paperwork, but the return may be a way to fund your whole dream. Programs include rebates, incentives, and financing. Rebates and incentives are the place to start. The **www.dsireusa.org** Database of State Incentives for Renewables and Efficiency lists, by state, all types of programs available from utilities, government, co-ops, and more. Programs like FHA Power Savers help us upgrade the home we have. Energy Upgrade Loans cover smaller projects from insulation to replacing your HVAC unit. Second mortgage loans are for larger renovations that include energy efficient elements. A PowerSaver first mortgage covers home purchase or refinance for energy efficiency improvements. If you want to do more than your home pro or financial resource is willing to help you do, don't give up. For different results, do something different.

Financing for your green home may be different from the usual home project and deserves extra consideration. Working with lenders and appraisers that understand the added value of a green home helps you get appraisals and loans that support the project. Many lenders and appraisers have not yet gotten the training and experience for appraising and financing green home projects. The Appraisal Institute has published the Green Appraisal Addendum to help appraisers track and assess the additional features of a green home or project.

Look around for the right bank. Some of them, like the Associated Bank, specialize in construction loans and lend their own money. They are more likely to have flexibility in how they underwrite their borrowers, the interest rates they offer, and their appraisal process. Look for ones that have built up a portfolio of green homes and gained valuable experience from these projects. Associated Bank is primarily a Midwest bank and their offerings are available in select states. All types of home projects may qualify for green consideration—new construction, renovations to a home just purchased, existing home renovations, and refinance. If you can list your long-term goals for your home, especially if you wish to live there a long time, you help the loan officer match the right offerings to your needs.

Green Insurance, Warranties, and Energy Guarantees

Many insurers now offer discounts for energy efficient homes and vehicles. Check with your homeowner insurance company and your auto insurance company to see if you qualify. For more information, check out the Insurance Information Institute at **www.iii.org**.

Homeowner's Insurance

Insurers promote sustainable building practices by offering green homeowners special pricing on policies. Special discounts are given for homes that meet stringent efficiency and sustainability standards, for example, LEED or NGBS certified homes. Once again you see the importance of maintaining your records and certification documents.

Coverage to replace/rebuild after a loss with more eco-friendly materials is often offered as an endorsement to a standard homeowners policy. Some companies pay homeowners extra if they replace old appliances with new Energy Star rated ones and when they recycle rather than send materials to the landfill.

If you generate power using solar, geothermal, or wind and sell the surplus to the local power company, some policies will cover the income you lose if your power goes out because of a covered peril. They also cover the extra expense of having to buy electricity from another source until your system is repaired.

Vehicle Insurance

Hybrid vehicles may qualify for discounts up to 10%. Some policies provide you the option to commit to upgrading to a similar model hybrid vehicle if your current auto is totaled. If your car uses a green fuel, such as electricity, natural gas, hydrogen, or ethanol, you might be eligible for a discount. It pays to ask.

Residential Energy Guarantee Program

There is a program that guarantees you a certain level of energy efficiency in your new home. Check out the website for the Residential Energy Guarantee program from Bonded Builders Warranty Group (**www.bondedbuilders.com/builders/products/residential-energy-guarantee/**). The program is available to builders who construct and certify homes that meet industry standards for energy efficiency such as HERS, Energy Star, LEED, or National Green Building Standard. It backs up their claims with dollars—you save on energy costs or they pay. Homeowners will be reimbursed for the cost of gas and electricity usage exceeding the home's predicted energy usage by more than 15%. Along with more traditional home warranty programs, the Residential Energy Guarantee rounds out the offerings for green home builders and is a program that offers benefits for you, the homeowner, and for your builder—and for the environment! Again, a win-win-win.

Resources

• • •

Bonded Builders Warranty Group—residential energy guarantee for homeowners
www.bondedbuilders.com

Chart comparing LEDS, CFLs, and incandescent bulbs
www.designrecycleinc.com/led%20comp%20chart.html

Cradle to Cradle Products Innovation Institute
www.c2ccertified.org

Database of State Incentives for Renewables and Efficiency (programs available from utilities, government, co-ops, and more)
www.dsireusa.org

Earth911—a community that helps consumers live in a more environmentally-friendly way, includes resources for hard to recycle items and work toward a zero-waste lifestyle.
www.Earth911.com

U.S. Department of Energy
www.Energy.gov
A wealth of information for saving energy, money, and time, including:
- *air conditioners*
- *appliance energy calculator*
- *Energy Star appliances*
- *heating systems, check out the Energy Saver 101 infographic*
- *Home Performance with Energy Star (HPwES) locate qualified energy auditors*
- *laundry energy saving tips*
- *windows*
- *window coverings*
- *Zero Energy Ready Home builders' challenge house designs*

U.S. Department of Energy Home Energy Yardstick
www.EnergyStar.gov

Calculate your home energy use
www.EnergyUseCalculator.com

Environmental Protection Agency's WaterSense Program
www3.epa.gov/watersense

Environmental Working Group—consumer information site
www.ewg.org

Greenpeace and Kimberly Clark
www.greenbiz.com/blog/2014/10/06/kimberly-clark-and-ngos-building-sustainable-supply-chain

Green Guard—List of low-emitting products for your home
www.greenguard.org

Green Home Coach—My website
www.greenhomecoach.com

Grean Seal—Information on green household products, construction materials, paints, printing and writing paper, household paper products, food packaging, hand soap and cleaners, cleaning services, and personal care products.
www.greenseal.org

Holiday LED lights
www.HolidayLEDs.com

Graphic of how much energy is wasted by appliances
www.homeenergysaver.ning.com

Homenav—My website
www.HomeNav.com

Home Tips for Women—Tina Gleisner's website
www.hometips4women.com

NASA Study on Using Plants to Clean Indoor Air
http://tinyurl.com/gu7g8a4

Office Essentials—A green office supplier with toilet paper made from recycled content
www.ofess.com

Union of Concerned Scientists—Consumer information site
www.ucsusa.org